Walk in Courage:

Trusting the Whispers of Your Intuition

Kim Beam

Defining Moments Press

REVIEWS OR TESTIMONIALS:

"Walk in Courage: Trusting the Whispers of Your Intuition is an incredible book filled with personal stories of struggling to find your intuition. Kim explains the steps in listening to your intuition as well as how to detect if it's going against your intuition. Included are meditation instructions that are incredibly helpful for someone just starting out on this path. Insightful, positive, and fun!"

~Nicole Mathias, Co-host on Generation X Paranormal Podcast, www.gxparanormal.com

"Kim Beam is the REAL DEAL."

~ **Sanjay Raja, Executive Producer and Host of** *Recipe for Wellness* **airing on PBS and Jen Brown Life Coach to Teens and Young Adults**

"Kim Beam is a breath of fresh air and so giving. Helping people find their light…, direction, and sometimes it's just a word that resonates with you and gives you clarity."

~**Kelly Bowley, Living Well with Kel**

"Kim, you're powerful. You're really very, very powerful. And empathetic."

~**Beth Jones, Trauma Mentor, and Best-Selling Author of** *Becoming an Empowered Survivor: You, Too, Can Heal From Trauma and Abuse*

"[Meeting Kim Beam] is really a life-changing experience and I can't say that enough."

~ **Brooklyn Calloway, Creator of BrookieLynn's Bungalow**

Defining Moments Press, Inc.

Copyright © Kim Beam, 2024. All rights reserved.

No part of this book may be reproduced in any form without permission in writing from the author.
For more information, visit KimBeam.com

Disclaimer: No part of this publication may be reproduced or transmitted in any form or by any means, mechanical or electronic, including photocopying or recording, or by any information storage and retrieval system, or transmitted by email without permission in writing from the author.

Neither the author nor the publisher assumes any responsibility for errors, omissions, or contrary interpretations of the subject matter herein. Any perceived slight of any individual or organization is purely unintentional.

Brand and product names are trademarks or registered trademarks of their respective owners.

Defining Moments ™ is a registered Trademark

Cover Design: Jack Oniel
Editing and Formatting: Leah Spelt L-I-G-I-A/Formatter: Sophie Hanks

Unlock Your Inner Potential: Free Audio Meditations Gift!

Are you ready to transform your life and connect with your inner self like never before? Dive into a world of peace, clarity, and personal growth with our exclusive gift—free audio meditations designed to guide you on your journey to self-discovery and empowerment!

🎁 What's Included:
- A Collection of Seven Guided Meditations: Each meditation is expertly crafted to help you relax, find balance, and tap into your inner wisdom.
- Breath Awareness Techniques: Learn to calm your mind and body with simple yet effective breath and body awareness techniques.
- Visualization Practices: Powerful methods to manifest your dreams and goals with clarity and intention.

✨ Why You Need This:
- Stress Reduction: Experience profound relaxation and relief from daily stress, helping you maintain a calm and centered state of mind.
- Enhanced Focus: Improve your concentration and mental clarity, allowing you to tackle your goals with renewed energy.
- Emotional Healing: Address and release past traumas and emotional blockages, paving the way for inner peace and personal growth.
- Spiritual Connection: Deepen your connection with your higher self and intuition, guiding you towards a more fulfilling and purpose-driven life.

💡 Why This Gift is Essential:

- Convenience: Enjoy these meditations anytime, anywhere, right from your smartphone. Whether you're at home, at work, or on the go, you have instant access to inner calm.
- Expert Guidance: Benefit from Kim's wisdom, her years of training with expert meditators, as a qualified Mindfulness Instructor, and a daily meditation practitioner. *The meditations included are not "Mindfulness Meditations"; they are meant to take you on a journey within yourself with care and expertise.*
- Free Access: Just click the link below and start your journey to a more peaceful and empowered you!

📖 How to Get Your Free Gift:

Simply click https://wic-meditation.kimbeam.com to claim your free audio meditations. Start experiencing the benefits today and open the door to a more balanced, centered, and empowered life.

Ready to enhance the journey presented in *Walk in Courage: Trusting the Whispers of Your Intuition*?
Click here and let the transformation begin!

Or scan the QR Code for instant access:

Dedication

To my teachers on this journey.

For the ones who may not have known they were guiding me along the way:

Jeffrey Allan, Chris Duncan, Esther and Jerry Hicks with Abraham, Regan Hillyer, Missy and Jon Butcher, Vishen Lakhiani, Heather Alice Shea, Bob Stahl, Jon Kabat Zinn, Gabby Bernstein,

And the ones who did:

Erin Dolan, Cami Foerester, Mimi Foerester, Linda Buckalew, Shannon Dimichele, Ann Marton, Brian Zimmerman, Katie Johnson, Bruce Latshaw, Kathy Baldwin, Cristina Leeson, Christine Ellis, Jamie Dawn,
Carolyn Sundheim Nystrom,
Momski, Dadski,
and

Steve Buckalew.

You were a man without equal. I will always miss your laugh and sometimes I hear it in my mind, in the background, just around the corner. You were so brave, going up to strangers in WaWa parking lots, stepping into their space, and saying, "I have a word from the Lord for you." You were always so encouraging, so open to hearing my doubts and fears, and so understanding about my insecurities—for you had them too. You saw my potential. You saw who I could be if I shed some of my hurts and traumas. You defended me. You championed my intuition abilities to hear and see for others. Thank you for investing so much of yourself in my development. I miss you.
Deeply.

Table of Contents

Acknowledgments 9
Pre-Words 11
Introduction 13
Chapter One: Will You Let Fear Stop You? 17
    Exercise 1: Meditation to Drop Fear 24
    Exercise 2: Meditation to Open the Vortex/Field 27
Chapter Two: The Power of Your Emotions 31
    Exercise 3: Meditation to Grow a Small Positive
    Feeling into Something Bigger 48
    Exercise 4: Grounding Meditation 50
Chapter Three: Truths About Intuition 53
Chapter Four: How to Enter into Your Intuition 71
Chapter Five: Asking for Signs and Automatic Writing 83
    Exercise 5: Meditation for Preparing to Automatic Write ... 94
Chapter Six: What to Do When You Get It "Wrong" 97
    Exercise 6: Meditation to Talk to a Guide/Spirit
    About Any Burning Life Question 103
Chapter Seven: Application and Why
There's a Need to Know Your Intuition 107
Chapter Eight: Living Intuitively and Boldly—The Wrap-Up ... 115
    Exercise 7: Meditation for a Dream of an Ideal Future ... 117
About the Author 121
Share Your Thoughts: Leave a Review! 123
ABOUT DEFINING MOMENTS PRESS 125
DEFINING MOMENTS BOOK PUBLISHING 127

Acknowledgments

To my amazing support team, in no particular order:

- **Dinyar Chavda**—Your honesty means everything to me.
- **John Artinger**—From day one, all those years ago, you believed me and the fact that you are still my cheerleader and in my corner means everything to me. Thank you.
- **Nicole Mathias of Generation X Paranormal**—Your encouragement and support have been so kindly given. Thank you.
- **Dave Spahl**—I think I've known you the longest of anyone I am close to—outside my family, that is—now that I think about it. Your support and friendship mean so much to me. Thank you for the honesty, the support, the regular feedback, and your belief in me.
- **Mary Masek**—You make my days at the hospital a delight. Thank you for the support you gave on this book and that you give daily when we work together. You make me laugh—so hard. I appreciate that more than you know.
- **Kelly Bowley of Living Well with Kel**—I am beyond excited to be able to call you one of my best friends. I love that we have connected as we have, that **April Pertuis, of Lightbeamers and The Speak Easy**, put us together as partners in crime.

- **Melanie Warner and the Defining Moments team**—Thank you so much for the support, the container to make all of this happen, and your willingness to help so many create their big visions into a reality.
- **Leah Spelt Ligia**—I am so, so grateful to have had you as my editor. From the crying texts I sent on a Friday night in the grocery store and to the level of understanding you bring to "getting me." Thank you. I don't have words for how grateful I am that it was *you* who helped me get to the finish line on this one.

Pre-Words

Let me hit pause here before I even start talking at all, and deal with an issue that is an inherent struggle when talking about anything metaphysical. Let's talk about what I call Source. It's *the word* that is the problem—not what it represents. We metaphysical types cannot seem to agree on the word we use.

What is Source when I say it to you, dear reader? Is it God? The Universe? Guides? Basic energy? What if someone is tapping into Angels or Stardust? We all use these words interchangeably to mean the same thing and every book I read on the subject has this same discussion in it—what am I going to call that nameless, faceless, beneficent, and compassionate guidance that comes in when every one of us is open to it?

I like Source because that is individually defined—what is your Source of guidance? Who in the spirit realms do you tap into when you are looking for answers or the information you are craving? I have a friend who calls it the Divine—but I struggle with God and religion. To say I have religious issues would be an understatement and the word "Divine" smacks of God and organized religion. Angels are too limiting. The Universe is too big and impartial. Guides are good, but sometimes I think my intuition is getting ideas from something bigger than Guides and Guides are not something everyone is able to subscribe to. But we all have a Source, I think. Whatever that is—my higher self, God, Spirit, the Universe. Whatever works for you—that is what Source means, even if the Source is just where the nameless, faceless, beneficent, and compassionate guidance comes from, with no other definition than that. You get to define it and you get to work with it how you will. It's your Source after all.

Introduction

I want to bring you into my history, into everything I have learned about intuition thus far in my life. Only I don't think I can fit all of it into the scope of this book. My goal is to be helpful to you, for you to learn how to trust your intuition and to move forward with confidence, knowing you are walking in your true purpose.

I have studied under pastors, intuitives, energy workers, breath healers, Reiki masters, and other teachers. I am a licensed clinical social worker in Pennsylvania and a certified educator in Massachusetts, Maryland, and Pennsylvania. But it was not my formal education that helped me to grow intuitively. It was working with my mentors, and working with other people's guiding practices that have shown me how to walk in my intuition.

But more than that, it has been my own work with my team, spirit, Source that has trained me up the most. I had a mentor who brought me through, brought me deep, brought me in, and helped me to trust my own inner voice. Without that mentor, I would not be where I am today. However, that mentor is not in my life anymore. He has crossed over this veil into the next. For years now, I have been learning from other energy workers, teachers, but also from what some might call spirit guides or Source in general. I have been learning from my own spiritual team that no one else can see or hear.

IMPORTANT NOTE: So, this is a channeled work.

What does that mean?

To write this book, I sat, listened, tapped in, and spoke out what I received from Source in order to write what I hope to be a helpful instructional guide that allows you, dear reader, to step in and start hearing and trusting your own intuition. I am reaching beyond myself, up into Source, to hear and sense and flow for you. It is my hope that you will be able to feel the difference in this writing, that it feels supported and bolstered by Source.

As you read, you may notice the tone of the book shifts inside each chapter—from my professional voice at the beginning and end of each chapter giving an introduction and a summary, to a collective "we"—which is Source speaking, and then there is an "I"—which is my own personal voice. Source calls me "Kim" as I was taking their words and sharing them. This is intentional and reflects the multidimensional guidance that came through during the writing process. Each voice carries its own energy and message, designed to help you hear, trust, and act on your own intuition.

This book is not just a collection of thoughts and ideas, but an instructional guide meant to encourage you, dear reader, to open yourself up to your own inner wisdom, just as I have done. The insights and exercises here are for you to step into your own power, supported by the same Source that guided me in creating this work.

At times, Source takes the content and expresses it freely. Other times in the writing, I sensed that I should take over and tell an anecdote from my own life. You, dear reader, will see the flow between me and Source. I hope that is not confusing to you.

I would like you to know, that before every writing session I did for this book, I started with the same prayer:

> "In this place, I welcome our highest selves, Source, angels, spirit guides, the superconscious, and any other sources of light (like our heart wisdom) that are working for our highest good.
>
> "I ask the spiritual team for wisdom and insight, illuminating dark places, and healing deep wounds.
>
> "We dedicate this time to be centered around our highest good to elevate our vibrations, and bring us into a space wherein we co-create lives we love.
>
> "May this journey, this time, this day, and these moments be a delight, a joy, and absolute yes! and huh-zah!"

There are meditations for most chapters to help you practice the concepts that are presented. In becoming a qualified mindfulness instructor, I was taught repeatedly that mindfulness and meditation are experiential practices. I have come to realize this is true for learning intuition too. It was a hard-won victory at times. I want to make it so much easier for you.

Being taught with words how to do what is in this book isn't enough—you have to put it into practice. Therefore, the meditations are here to help guide you through the lessons.

I recorded the meditations and then transcribed them verbatim. Only reading the verbatim transcript didn't always make sense and didn't flow as a written text should. Therefore, I have edited them slightly to make them more natural to read. So, there are differences between the spoken meditations and the written ones, but that is only for stylistic purposes.

The meditations can be found here:
http://wic-meditation.kimbeam.com/

Chapter One

Will You Let Fear Stop You?

Welcome to Chapter One. Breath is life. It's the very first action we take when entering this world and the last as we depart. With every inhale, we welcome the possibility of growth, and with every exhale, we release what no longer serves us. This rhythm of breath is essential, yet so often we overlook its power. I have witnessed the first and last breaths of life and know deeply the significance of this sacred cycle.

In this chapter, we'll explore how subconscious programming can keep us stuck—trapped by routine, fear, and resistance. Joe Dispenza and Heather Alice Shea both suggest that much of our daily lives are run by automatic habits that work to keep us "safe." Yet, the truth is, our subconscious fears anything that is different, labeling new opportunities as dangerous—even when the new opportunities are our heart's deepest desires. The question becomes: will you allow fear to keep you in the comfort of the familiar, or will you choose to press beyond your Jericho Walls?

I have learned to move past my fear-based programming through meditation and visualization, creating space for new possibilities. By entering what some call "The Vortex" or "The Field," I have transformed my life, and so can you. In this chapter, we'll dive into the tools and methods I use—techniques that anyone can learn—to break free from fear, to step into courage, and to begin designing the life you envision.

As this is a channeled work, we will refer to Kim as "Kim" and ourselves as "we." Kim likes to say it starts with breath. She had a revelation a couple of years ago when her father died. At that time, Kim worked in a hospital. She worked with moms and babies and had experienced new life in the sense that she was standing in the hallway when a new baby was born. The first thing a new baby does is inhale and the last thing a body does when the spirit leaves the planet is it exhales.

Life begins with an inhale and ends on an exhale. Breath is life.

Joe Dispenza in his book, *Breaking the Habit of Being Ourselves,* states that most of a person's actions are based on subconscious automatic programming. The body does what the body does and the brain is sort of asleep. This can be proven when you get up in the morning and you do the same thing without thinking. This can be proven when driving to work and you are forced off your normal path because of a detour and you become irrationally angry. This can be proven when your brain decides to go on a diet and your body starts to think all these thoughts about how it's being starved. Subconscious Automatic Programming guides our lives and our destiny. Being in a rut is comfortable.

Chapter One

Heather Alice Shea and her program *True Intuition* states, the subconscious has one job. One job alone. That one job is to keep you safe. It doesn't matter what the danger is. It can be seen only as a perceived danger and not an actual danger. The truth is your subconscious sees anything that's different as dangerous.

So, stepping out into your intuition isn't going to be easy. Every cell in your body is being driven by your subconscious. And your subconscious says, "NOOOO!" to anything that is out of the realm of everyday life for you. It doesn't matter what the change is—asking somebody on a date, quitting your job for a new job, buying a new house, or starting a business venture that will leave the comfort of working for someone else.

Anything that's out of the norm of every day in-and-out routine life is scary and your subconscious' job is to stop anything that's scary and to keep you safe. So, you are fighting internal programming any time you do something that is out of your current routine. Again, your subconscious keeps you in a rut. It keeps you stuck.

There are two methods that Kim uses to move herself when she feels she is stuck or in a rut. Kim has found that it is not easy to change her programming—that she has to do her work in order to change her mindset and circumstances to create a better setup for herself.

She has stepped in and stepped out and uses her meditation skills and intuition in order to create newness in her life. She has spent hours on meditation cushions stepping into Source and pressing into what is not seen yet in her own life. By pressing in with her mind into what she would like to experience in this lifetime, she helps to create those details in her present physical reality. She uses the possibility of maybe and the feeling of hope to get her subconscious comfortable with what is a potential to be seen in the physical. She creates what is physical here on Earth by stepping into the potential inside her imagination in meditation. She enters the space that Abraham Hicks calls "The Vortex," what Joe Dispenza calls "The Field," what Chris Duncan calls "Infinite Possibility" or "Innocence."

Kim envisions a new space within the Vortex, imagining her ideal life as if it is happening in reality. She imagines all the details, particulars, colors, and experiences. If she's dreaming of her dream home, she not only imagines what it looks like outside, but where it is located on Earth—imagining a sunset and its location right on a beach. Sometimes she will choose a room, like the kitchen and what the kitchen island looks like in relation to the refrigerator. By cultivating a sense of openness and spaciousness within herself, she creates room for these desired experiences to enter her life naturally, with grace and flow.

This is something the average person can learn to do. It's easy if you are willing to learn. Creating openness and space is easy once you relax into it. It is something that takes practice and a willingness. The average person is not able to just create by thinking. There is too much resistance. There are too many thoughts and fears and blockages that stop the thoughts from flowing in and, as a result, you spend more time thinking about what is not possible than what is possible. Or you think more about what you do not want than what you do want. For things that are highly charged and things you really want, your emotions block you from receiving them.

Intuition helps to create avenues where you are able to walk through the walls of resistance. Intuition is able to tell you where there is a soft spot in the resistance wall that is able to be pressed open to help you see your way through to a path. Before intuition spoke, that path felt completely blocked. The more you spend time in meditation and listening to your intuition, the easier it becomes to push on soft spots in resistance walls. Eventually, you will just bring down the resistance wall all together.

In the Bible, there is a story about the wall of Jericho where the people walked around the wall seven times, screamed, and the wall came down. That's a little bit of a simplified version of the story, to be honest.

In your own lives, you have created your own Jericho Walls—walls that feel solid, massive, and immoveable. You came by these walls honestly. They are there to keep you safe. However, these walls are also made up of the lies you believe—you have to have the right education, the right internships, the right experiences, to know the right people, to live in the right part of the world. Go ahead, take a moment—what are the massive, solid Jericho Walls around you right now that are stopping you from moving into what you see as your current dream?

Seriously. Think about that for a moment.

Whether that Jericho Wall is there to keep you safe, or to keep other people safe, these walls feel like absolute fact. In reality, they are a construct made up by your mind and this world you live in. The truth is, this resistance wall, which we have just named Jericho, can fall with a little faith and effort.

This wall is stopping the good things from flowing in. Kim likes to say this is when she gets resisty. When the walls come up, you experience emotional resistance. You are resisty when you are not feeling like there is flow between you and the thing you want. You are resisty when you recognize that something is blocking you. You are especially resisty when you feel blocked and so you start to emotionally press back and fight against what is blocking you.

Another truth?

All resistance is rooted in the emotion of fear. The thing that is blocking you is fear.

Fear is not something to just stare at and allow. Fear can be overcome. Fear is a natural human reaction. Please do not be ashamed to feel fear. If you are human and you are doing new things, you will experience fear. It's what you do to move the fear that matters. It's what you do to create courage in the presence of fear that matters.

If you squash the fear down, push it down inside the body, it will just congeal in the hip structure of the body—where all negative emotion goes to hide when it's pushed down. Someone who has anxiety or panic attacks? Their torso is so full of fear it's no longer able to be contained. It comes spilling out and over, like an overfull glass.

So, let's talk a little about the unpopular subject of fear in a way that makes it fun, light, and helpful. In *Harry Potter and the Prisoner of Azkaban*, Professor Lupin is teaching his third years how to manage a Boggart—a creature in *Harry Potter* that turns into the thing you fear the most. When the Boggart turns on Harry, Professor Lupin gets in the way and draws the Boggart's attention away from Harry onto himself. Professor Lupin later said that he expected the Boggart to turn into He-Who-Must-Not-Be-Named. Harry said, in essence, "I'm more scared of a Dementor than a Voldemort." Dementors are giant, black cloaked, cold, dark beings that suck all the happiness out of the world. Lupin is both surprised and impressed and says as much. Lupin concedes Harry is afraid of fear—not death. Lupin calls Harry wise to be more afraid of fear than anything else in this world.

Fear is part of the human condition. If you are human, breathing in and out, then fear is a part of your existence. You must learn to manage your fear if you are to grow. Fear is a natural

Chapter One

and normal reaction to anything new. It is also the root of all that keeps you stuck. It is at the root of all that keeps you where you are, and keeps you from all the potential of who and what you could become.

If you want to excel and create a life you love, by stepping into your intuition to see where that path will take you, we will need to help you drop your fear. Remember, fear is just an emotion. Just like any other emotion, fear comes in and it goes out. It won't last very long. The amount of power you give to any emotion is in relation to how much resistance you give to it or the amount you feed it. Resistance feeds the emotions you don't like by pushing them away and making them stronger. The more resistance you give to a negative emotion, the bigger it becomes. The more you release and allow the negative emotion, the smaller it becomes. Emotions create your reality. We will discuss this in the next chapter.

Fear is often the unseen barrier that keeps us from moving forward. It's a natural part of life, but it doesn't have to control us. By recognizing and managing fear, and embracing tools like meditation and visualization, you can begin to dismantle the walls that hold you back. Now that you've learned how fear operates within your mind and body, you're equipped to take your first steps toward change.

But fear isn't the only thing that influences your path. Emotions, in general, are powerful forces that shape our reality. In the next chapter, we'll delve into how you can harness the power of your emotions—particularly those beyond fear—to create the life you truly desire.

Thank you for joining me on this journey.

Exercise 1: Meditation to Drop Fear

I invite you to find a comfortable seated position. If you're sitting cross-legged on the floor, that's great. If you're seated in a chair, simply place your feet on the floor. And if you're lying down, that's okay too—just be aware that lying down might make you feel sleepy. Choose the position that allows you to stay alert and present.

This meditation is designed to help you release fear. As we've discussed in the chapter, fear is a normal human experience, deeply rooted in our instinct for self-preservation. Your subconscious is wired to protect you and fear plays a big role in that.

Now, I want you to imagine yourself in a place you absolutely love—a place where you feel completely safe. For me, this place is the beach, but your safe place might be in the mountains, your home, or a cherished spot from your childhood. Wherever it is, picture yourself there now, fully immersed in the safety and comfort of this environment.

Next, visualize a backpack. This could be a backpack from your childhood or simply the first one that comes to mind. Typically, backpacks are worn on your back, but I want you to imagine taking it off your shoulders and wrapping it around to the front of your chest, as if you're hugging it. Feel the weight of the backpack resting against your chest, your arms through the loops, and the straps around your back.

Now, imagine that this backpack contains all of your fears—big or small. These could be major fears, like the fear of illness, or smaller fears, like a fear of spiders. Whatever fears come to mind, place them in this backpack. Take your time with this; there's no rush. Breathe in deeply, and as you exhale, continue to place any fears that arise into the backpack.

Chapter One

If you remember more fears later, know that you can always return to this safe space, add them to the backpack, and continue with this process.

When you're ready, visualize a fire in front of you. It could be a campfire on the beach, a fire pit in the mountains, or simply a small flame. Now, imagine that the flames are turning purple—a powerful, transformative color. Take a deep breath in, and as you exhale, notice the purple flames.

Now, gently remove the backpack from your chest. As you do, you're disconnecting it from your heart space, one of the most vulnerable and protected areas of your body. Carefully place the backpack into the purple flames.

You may notice cords, attachments, or lines connecting your heart to the backpack. These represent your ties to the fears inside. To sever these connections, you can imagine using any tool that resonates with you—a pair of scissors, a sword from Archangel Michael, or even a bolt of lightning from Zeus. The important thing is to feel that the cords are fully cut and that the attachments are burned away in the purple flame.

Take a moment to watch as the backpack and its contents burn away, transforming into ash. If you need more time, feel free to pause here.

When you're ready, visualize the flames extinguishing. Now, imagine sifting through the cool ashes. Just like an airplane's black box, there's an indestructible box within these ashes. Reach out, find this box, and open it. Inside, you'll discover a gift—something that your fear has given you. This could be a lesson, an insight, or a newfound strength that has come from facing and releasing your fear.

Take a moment to express gratitude for this gift, for this time, and for the process of releasing your fear. Now, check in with your body. Do you feel lighter or heavier? If you feel heavier, consider repeating this meditation. If you feel lighter, you might still choose to do it again to release even more.

    Thank you for allowing me to share this practice with you.

Chapter One

Exercise 2: Meditation to Open the Vortex/Field

Before we begin, let's take a moment to understand what the vortex is and why we want to enter it. The vortex is a state of alignment with your highest self, where your energy resonates with the frequency of your desires and the Universe's flow. In the vortex, you are in harmony with your true nature, allowing you to easily attract and manifest what you seek. It's a place of pure potential, where everything you want is within reach and all possibilities are open to you.

Find a comfortable and safe seated position where you can close your eyes and fully relax. It's important to remember that this process can take time and practice. For some, like Kim, it took many sessions before she truly felt like she was entering the vortex, even if it was only during the last few minutes of meditation. Others might find themselves in the vortex almost immediately. Wherever you are on this journey, know that it's okay.

Now, let's begin by focusing on your breath. Take a deep breath in, and then exhale. When we say "find your breath," we mean to notice where you feel it most in your body. Is it at your nostrils? In the rise and fall of your chest? Or maybe in your belly? Simply observe where your breath is most present without trying to change it. Let your breath be as it is.

Now, shift your attention to the center of your chest, or perhaps your belly. If your mind begins to wander, which is completely normal, gently bring your focus back to your breath and body. There's no need to judge the distractions—just acknowledge the thoughts and return to your meditation.

Focus on your breath for a couple of moments.

Next, I want you to imagine a wide-open space. It could be a field, a vast desert, or any place that feels expansive and safe for you. If a field doesn't resonate, choose a space from your past where you felt a sense of openness and peace.

In this space, imagine standing still. Now, stretch your awareness as far as you can, as if you had arms that could extend endlessly. Feel your energy expanding out into the space around you, reaching farther and farther. As you do this, know that your energy field is expanding too, growing into this vast, open area.

As your energy extends, breathe in hope, joy, delight, excitement, and the possibility of yes—any feelings we didn't name that makes you feel whole. Know that we are doing this with you, creating this expansive space of potential together.

As you continue to expand your energy, visualize yourself stepping into the vortex, this state of pure alignment. Feel the shift of energy—feel how open it is, how wide the space, how vast the possibilities.

Imagine this space as full of infinite potential, where anything is possible.

Once you are sure you are in this space, begin to visualize all the good things you want to bring into your life. It could be financial abundance, a dream home, a car, or even the loving relationships you wish to cultivate. See these desires taking shape in this open space, within the vortex.

Picture what your life would look like when all this goodness flows in—how your home, your family, and your daily experiences will change. Feel the joy and excitement of these possibilities as you hold them in your mind.

This space may take practice to fully create, and that's perfectly fine. The more time you spend in the vortex, the more natural it will feel, and the easier it will become to access this state of alignment. If you wish, stay here a little longer, allowing yourself to bask in the limitless potential where everything is a "yes" and anything is possible. When you're ready, you can continue your day, but feel free to stay as long as you'd like.

Chapter Two

The Power of Your Emotions

Let's dive into the emotional landscape that forms the foundation of your intuition. Emotions are more than fleeting feelings; they are powerful enough to create the reality you are currently living. In this chapter, we'll explore a tool called the "Polarity of Feelings Line," which helps you understand where you are emotionally and how to shift from negative emotions to positive ones. You'll learn that emotions are not just reactions to life—they're part of how you manifest your reality and how you tap into the wisdom of your intuition.

    Here we'll look at how to work with your emotions deliberately. By mastering your feelings and moving up the Polarity of Feelings Line, you'll create the emotional space needed to receive intuitive insights clearly and effectively. Together, we'll practice techniques to transform negative emotions into positive energy, allowing you to elevate your emotional state and bring clarity into your life.

Emotions are so important. Kim was first introduced to the importance of emotions through Esther and Jerry Hicks and the need to reach for a better feeling thought. By working on your inner thought life, you create your current reality. If you want to know what your thoughts in the past felt like, take a look at the reality you are currently living. How does it feel? Well, your past emotions created this current reality.

Kim struggled with anxiety for years. She had panic attacks in airports where she would have to run to the bathroom in order to be sick. She was on an SSRI (anti-anxiety medication) while teaching in the schools, because the amount of pressure was just more than her frame could handle.

Her thoughts followed what she calls negatively swirling patterns. For Kim, her negatively swirling patterns circle or cycle around her anxiety thoughts. She would think thoughts that made her more anxious, that would lead to more anxious thoughts. She would dream up negative "what if" scenarios: what if there's a school shooting? What if I get yelled at by the principal—again? What if this parent gets mad at me and lies about me to the superintendent—again?

Then there were days when students would make her anxiety soar. The days when they would ask if she would be willing to take a bullet for them. Or they would ask questions that were of real concern, but weren't necessarily things an English teacher should be addressing—sex, dating, divorce, suicidal thoughts, miscarriage, abuse at home, and teenage pregnancy—but were things that came up because Kim was that kind of teacher. Kim would push her anxiety away and be present with her students who needed her presence. She would also report their circumstances to guidance, the state, the principals—and it was the telling of their stories to someone else that often brought on Kim's panic attacks—the feeling of betrayal the students may feel because Kim was a mandatory reporter, and keeping them safe was not necessarily keeping their secrets.

Reaching for a "better feeling thought" allows for more regulated emotions and perspectives. If Kim had known about reaching for a better feeling thought in these scenarios, she would have been able to have a different perspective on making a child-line report, instead of thinking, "What if this child thinks I'm betraying them?" She would have been focusing on, "By telling the truth, we are getting this child help. By revealing this person's suicidal thoughts, I am protecting them from themselves."

Now, when Kim starts to think, "What if I fail?," she thinks, "If I don't try, I will have failed. It's the trying that is success," which gives her motivation to keep pressing in toward her goal.

When Kim started the practice of reaching for a better feeling thought, she was working in the hospital under a boss who didn't support her or even try to understand Kim's perspective. Kim worked hard to reach for better feeling thoughts in the midst of stressful workdays and a hostile work environment. Kim believes, because of the work of reaching for a "better feeling thought," she was offered a job she adored at a school as a school therapist. She got that job from a text message on her phone from a staffing agency she didn't even know she signed up with.

From that job, she took the summer to think about what she wanted and decided to work part time for the hospital while building herself as a brand. She held a podcast where a woman asked for an intuitive reading, and from that meeting, Kim wrote this book, and will be on PBS.

Kim fully believes by reaching for better feeling thoughts, she was the right vibrational match for opportunities to find her.

If you want your current reality to get better, think about thoughts that make you feel better. If you want a different future than the present you are currently living in, you have to create different feelings now. It might take some time to see the change in your circumstances, but the reality is when you work on your feelings and create better feelings, your circumstances will improve. This is law.

You may doubt us, but what do you have to lose? Keep thinking thoughts that make you feel bad and make you stay stuck in your current reality. Or, start reaching for thoughts that make you feel better, that lead to more thoughts that make you feel better, and then watch. Keep it up as practice. Kim didn't get to where she is quickly. She had to think better thoughts regularly for years and she has watched how things changed. Some things that came in were sudden, like the job offer, but others were over time, like the choice not to take a full-time position at the hospital and allowing herself the opportunity to fulfill the dream of being a keynote speaker and full-time author.

The Law of Polarity has its roots in the ancient Chinese symbol of the Yin and Yang. Yin being slow, calm, peaceful, waiting, watching and Yang being doing, active, fast, exuberant.

For Kim, the Law of Polarity applies to emotions. You can't be morose (which is a big word for super-sad) if you've never experienced being ecstatic (which is a big word for being super-joyful). You can't be infuriated if you haven't ever been calm, placid or serene.

Now here's the thing—these emotions are all on a line with each other.

But there are *many* words in between as you move from morose to ecstatic.

Chapter Two

Morose shifts up to melancholy, which shifts up to sad. Then you come to the middle with peace or contentment. Then if you keep moving up the Law of Polarity line, you come to cheerful, then joyful, then exuberant, then ecstatic (see the diagram just below). But please know, the words in between are examples. There are so many more words we can use between morose and ecstatic—we're giving just a few.

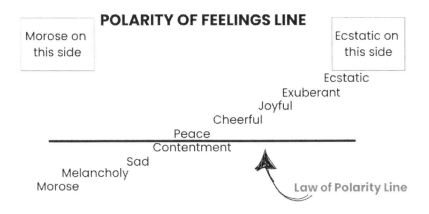

The great thing about the Polarity of Feelings is that it is custom-made with you in mind.

What emotions are your baseline emotions?

Kim had to work on this. She had to move out of melancholy, apprehension, and foreboding and trained herself to live in expectation, anticipation, excitement, joy, and exuberance. When she actively shifted her emotions, her expectations in life changed. Her vibration rose, and her general anxiety dropped.

When you have a negative emotion, it is often tied to a negative thought or a negative experience. If you are able to isolate those thoughts and where they originate, you are able to find the source of the bad feeling. As most people in the therapy world know, once you see the problem, it no longer has the same power over you. So, if you are able to look back and see what thoughts are causing the negative feeling, then you are able to find the source. Once you find the source, you can actively choose a "better feeling thought." You can deliberately choose a thought that makes you feel better.

Only you can decide when a thought makes you feel better. We could give suggestions of things that might make you feel better, but in reality, they have to sit in your body and resonate. The thoughts must be thoughts that fit you correctly if they are going to be powerful enough to make you feel better.

You have to create your own Polarity of Feelings Line based on your baseline level of feelings and where you want to move up to. Also, you may have a sad line, and you could have an anger/frustrated line. You can have a peaceful and calm line too, where you are working on creating even better feelings than contentment.

Kim, now that she has expectation, anticipation, excitement, joy, and exuberance down, is working on creating even better feelings as her baseline on her Polarity of Feelings. She notices thoughts that don't make her feel good and she does work to shift her thoughts to better feeling thoughts so her baseline of feelings moves up the Polarity of Feelings Line.

Often the things that cause distress are the negative things people say to you. It's so hard to let go of someone's negative words that hurt so deeply. They can also be the hardest to shift into a better feeling thought—since it came out of someone else's mouth about you, it must be true, right? So, let's see if we can help you shift those thoughts into something better.

Chapter Two

Dear reader, we want you to think of something that somebody actually said to you that you haven't been able to get out of your head.

Kim will give you an example to help you along.

A number of years ago, when I was in my second master's program, this time for Social Work, I went out to dinner with the woman who was married to my father for the last 25 years of his life. At this meal with just the two of us, to which she invited me, she corrected me for never offering to pay. I was in graduate school and didn't have any money—I couldn't afford the restaurants she invited me to. In fact, I couldn't even afford to live in my mother's house and pay "rent" by covering the utility bills.

At this dinner, the woman married to my father told me to my face that I wasn't a member of the immediate family. She stated that I didn't go on family trips with them, because, even though I was my father's daughter and she was married to my father, I was not a member of the immediate family. I wish I had a video of my face as she spoke these words. I really do. This moment caused some significant pain in my life, but I also made a decision that day. As a result of the statement, "You are not an immediate member of my family," I have made choices to help me feel better about who I am and how I fit into my own family dynamics. I worked on my relationship with my father, not with her. I did what I had to do in order to keep a close relationship with my father, in regard to her. Since my father's death (which I like to call "the big leave" or just "my dad left"), I have chosen to distance myself from this woman. I have chosen to not give her the power of making me feel bad anymore.

When I used to think of the sentence, "You are not a member of my immediate family," I used to cry. It would also make me mad.

I would be jealous of the trips they went on without me. I would be hurt all over again by the words.

Now, when I think of the words, "You are not a member of the immediate family," I think, "Thank goodness."

Thank goodness!

I look at the pain she has caused other people. I look at the fights that she has started and kept running. I look at the discord in her own life and I am grateful that I have distance and that this is not a story in my life anymore.

Is it painful for me still? Like when I see photos on social media of these people who used to be "family" having a Christmas without me? A little.

The reality is, I miss my father. That is what I miss. Not her. Not that story. Not those circumstances. I miss my dad.

Knowing I am free makes me feel free emotionally. I am not wrapped up in her and making her happy anymore. I am no longer tied to those circumstances and by celebrating that freedom, I move to the other side of the Polarity of Feelings line—from negative to positive.

These are not easy things to talk about.
These things are deeply painful.

To be honest, it took seven to eight years to gain enough perspective to start finding positive aspects in this life event—that's almost a decade of pain. I never gave up hope that one day I would find them. I just let this memory sit around, sometimes causing fights between me and my father, sometimes making me cry, and for reasons I won't get into, making me resent the word, "Italy." Only I didn't hate Italy; I was struggling with jealousy.

I never stayed stagnant though. I would bring these negative feelings to my meditation cushion. I would own them. I would cry. I would move them around and look at them. I would let them be—if they were sitting heavy in my chest, or in my throat. I would talk about them, make stupid jokes as if the hurt feelings and terrible situation were funny. I was fluid with my feelings, acknowledging and accepting I was hurt, allowing them to shift and change with time, knowing one day, the pain would fade. Knowing one day, I would find something positive about the whole situation.

There are ways to find positive perspectives on highly charged negative experiences. When you are able to open a negative experience to explore it for positive facets, you create an openness and flow that allows good things to enter your experience.

So go ahead and think about your painful moment that we asked you to think about above, that time someone said something that was deeply painful for you. What are some positives you can find in that moment? What is one thing—even if it's the size of a mustard seed—what is one small positive aspect that will help you shift your perspective to something slightly more positive? Then see if you can breathe into that positivity and make it grow a little. See if you can fill it up around you, just take that tiny positive thought—big as a mustard seed—and turn it into something so much bigger. (Did you know that the mustard seed grows into a tree? It's an herb, but it becomes a tree.) See if you can grow that good feeling thought to fill the whole bubble around you. We give you words for this at the end of the chapter and there is a recording in the meditations found at: http://wic-meditation.kimbeam.com/

For Kim, her positive emotions are the most important thing to her. She does whatever it takes to maintain positive emotions in her life. She works on her emotions all the time because she wants a life that is inspiring and exciting.

The more she can clear out negative emotions, press into positive emotions, and create openness and flow, the more she is connected to Source and her intuition.

To hear your intuition, you need to be in a flow state.

Negative emotions create attachment. People talk about forgiveness and letting go of negativity. People talk about the need to release negative emotions. So many people talk about their struggles with anger and jealousy. In the culture of the United States, so many people talk about managing their anger and letting negative emotions go.

You can also be holding onto positive emotions.

Some people are always chasing positive emotions and they start to wear a "false front." They wear a mask of kindness, or sweetness, or positivity. They do not cope with their negative emotions in ways that allow them to be at peace with themselves. They are putting on a fake persona that all is great and wonderful. This is a lie as well.

This situation also just squashes the negative emotions in the body, keeping them stuck in the body, only to settle into the lower hips.

Being your authentic self, working through negative emotions while pressing into more positive feelings and doing this in a way that is real, honest, and intentional is what creates change in your life.

In her mid-forties, Kim fell in love. For real this time. Not just what she thought was love. She fell in Walden Pond, overwhelm-your-senses, and vibrate-with-a-whole-other-frequency love. He asked to be let go, for his own reasons. Kim will never be the same again. Honestly, this powerful positive experience transformed her in so many ways. And to let it go? She didn't want to.

Some of the positive aspects of that relationship just felt so good. So, she remembers the good feelings and swims around them, for this relationship taught her so many new good feelings she hadn't experienced before. By intentionally being in those strong, powerful, positive feelings, she lifts her overall mood and creates better frequencies when she is struggling or sad. But she actually walks a fine line here. Sometimes, even without her really noticing until it's too late, the good feelings the relationship created actually turn to longing and pain because the connection has been severed.

Kim has had her moments of crying about this lost connection. But she also has now come to the point where she has released it and allowed him to be himself and her to be herself, which is best for both of them. She struggled to do that for a long time. While she was in the midst of that struggle, she chose to sit on the side of positive emotions. It was easy to fall into sadness, longing, and despair, and she did. In those moments, she would cry it out. But then, she would think about how good the highs with him were, how exciting and vibrant. We recognize how hard it is to be human and how hard it can be to remain positive when a connection has been lost. It's the effort of trying to be authentic, move negative emotions through the body, and focus on positive elements that makes all the difference.

When Kim was just out of college, living on the North Shore of Boston, she was sitting in the North Beverly Starbucks. The guy she super liked had just come in. She watched him and hoped he would come over and say, "Hi," to her.

One day, she confessed her crush to a friend. Kim told her friend that even though Kim really wanted there to be something between the two of them, Kim "liked him too much." She knew she was holding onto the crush and the hope of it becoming a reality too hard. Even back then, Kim instinctively knew about the Law of Attraction and the need to release and allow.

When her friend asked Kim to clarify what she meant about why it wouldn't work out between Kim and the Crush, Kim said, "I'm gripping onto it too tightly. I have to let it go."

Kim wasn't able to let it go; he chose someone else and married her.

Kim knew she was not steeping in positive emotions. She was on the negative side of the Polarity of Feelings. She was clinging to what she wanted; she was clinging to it too hard. What happened in reality is she pushed him away. The longing, the reaching, the grasping, the wanting made it so the opportunity got further and further away. Her holding onto the want and longing side of the Polarity of Feelings had the opposite effect of what she wanted. If she were able to open her hands, allow him to go his own way and release him, he may have turned to her instead. But that's not how it all worked out. She saw it for what it was, a good learning experience.

When Kim deeply desires something, she recognizes that her emotions can cloud her judgment. In these moments, she seeks out people whose intuition can help her see clearly when her own intuition is obscured by strong emotions.

She may be able to perceive clearly when it comes to other people's circumstances or even other situations in her own life. But when she's emotionally invested, it becomes difficult for her to see what she needs to do or to anticipate the potential outcomes of her decisions. When her emotions are too strong, she struggles to find her own path. In those moments, she needs space, time, and distance, as well as the wisdom that someone else's intuition can offer.

Being able to handle your emotions, knowing where you are on the Polarity of Feelings Line, being able to calibrate your emotions and shift from negative to positive emotions is necessary in order to get you into a balanced head space to be able to receive intuitive information. If you are not in the right emotional state to receive, messages will bounce off or you might misinterpret the information you are receiving.

Kim's favorite way to clear her head and get herself in a good emotional state is by grounding. This meditation practice can be done in a myriad of ways.

If you ever watched the movie, *Pretty Woman*, Julia Roberts' character has the Richard Gere character take off his socks and walk in the grass. This is really an excellent way to ground and get in touch with earth and the core of yourself. Kim's practice is a combination of Jeffrey Allen's *Duality* program and Heather Alice Shea's *True Intuition* grounding practice.

The point of grounding is really foundational for intuition.

Think of a tree. Trees need a root system in order to support the trunk, branches, and leaves. The root system is a solid foundation. The root system also looks a lot like the branches of the tree—as below, so above. As without, so within.

If the roots of the tree are solid, the branches can be blown all over in a hurricane or tornado and the tree will hold tight. The roots hold the whole system in place. So, no matter what chaos, what dervish, what overwhelm is happening in your life, the roots of your ability to ground will hold your core centered and your branches secure.

If you don't have the ability to ground, when you step into intuition, you get a little bit weird. You will have ideas that don't jive with reality and you will become more floaty and off. Kim likes to think Professor Sybill Trelawney, the Divination teacher in *Harry Potter,* really just needs to spend more time grounding.

To be clear, when you start knowing you are getting intuitive hits (we were going to say, when you start getting them—but you are getting them all the time, you just aren't calibrated to see them yet, maybe), even with grounding, you might feel like your ideas are "floaty," "wild," and "out there." Kim often checks in with psychics and other intuitives around her to make sure what she's getting resonates with them. For her, some of the ideas are so wild when compared to her reality, they don't seem possible or even plausible.

So, how do you ground?

Kim prefers to sit on a meditation cushion on her living room floor. She recognizes this is not what most people will do. You can sit in a chair or stand.

Heather Alice Shea, creator of Atmana, says to ground down into the core of the earth from the heart space. She also says, also from the heart space, to lift up high into the cosmos to find your highest self. The highest self is the "youiest you that ever you'd" as Heather likes to say.

Kim has found that she is not comfortable going down into the ground for grounding from her heart chakra; it feels too far away. She likes to ground from her root chakra which is the bottom of the pelvic bowl, the base of the pelvic floor, and the space that energetically houses security, safety, and contentment—basically the bottom two levels of Maslow's hierarchy of needs—food, water, shelter, clothing, safety, and security. Some people aren't comfortable with the pelvic floor or pelvic bowl—so she has them think about grounding from around their belly button area, which is the seat of creativity, emotions, and manifestation in the body.

She sends a rope down into the earth—one of those big thick ropes one finds on giant ships from the 1800s.

Jeffrey Allen in his *Duality* program takes grounding to the earth to a whole different level. Kim likes it. A lot. It makes her legs heavy. He says in his program that when someone grounds with him, they have to release the grounding cord when they are at the gym so they can box-jump. Otherwise, the grounding is so intense, they can't get even one foot off the ground, when they normally do the 2 ½ feet to 3 feet jump on top of the box. Jeffery Allen also just doesn't send the cord or rope, or bit of light. If you put out your arms to your sides and imagine a circumference line going all around you, he sends everything inside the circumference down into the core of the earth. He has you make a home down there; has you look at the magma, and get cozy.

Once Kim is good and grounded, she takes the same kind of thick rope from an 1800s ship and sends it up into the sky. Sometimes she uses light from the crown chakra, if she thinks the light will lock her in as tightly as the rope will. She sends it on up through the clouds, through the atmosphere, past the line that she imagines between our atmosphere and the universe's stars. She sends it up and deeper into the dark until she comes to Source. Whatever Source, whoever Source is for you. That could be the highest self, that could be angels, that could be God, that could be spirit, that could be you-name-it, but you tap in and that's where the information comes from.

So, you're rooted into the Earth on a very deep level and then you're rooted in above to gain as much information as possible. Once you are linked in above and you are rooted in down below, your orientation is no longer earthbound. Your orientation is now one who is looking for energy information for everyone's highest good and your body is poised to receive it.

You may even start meditation practice with that, "I am here for the highest good of all." Or "I am looking for my highest good." Or "I embrace Source's wisdom for the highest good." Whatever works and resonates for you.

These tools can be helpful to people, and any tool that works is valuable to have in your toolbox for difficult times. Kim's practice may not be the same as yours, and yours may not be the same as hers. You need to find what works for you. If you try to follow someone else's practice and it doesn't resonate with you, you're less likely to stick with it. You are also going to become resisty and it won't open the doors you are looking to open. You will become discouraged and give up. Then you won't have a practice at all.

If you find yourself in a space that is high energy and topsy-turvy, Jeffrey Allen has a method to ground physical space, not just your body. If you have a house of teenagers or young toddlers whose energy is rapidly shifting, or you live with a difficult roommate who messes with the energetic atmosphere, or you find that you yourself are changeable, Jeffrey Allen suggests grounding the corners of your house, the same way you ground yourself.

Kim has ground her office at the hospital where she works per diem. She has also found that grounding gets a little weird at times.

One of the two ways it gets weird is, her office at the hospital where she works as a social worker in the Care Coordination Department is on the 6th floor. When she grounds, she has to ground through six levels of building before she hits the earth. Sometimes, she just pretends she's directly on the earth. She figures the distance of her above the earth in relation to her distance to the center of the earth is negligible from that perspective. But from her human perspective, six floors are kind of high up to pretend they don't exist. Living in the two perspectives can be challenging.

The other way grounding gets weird: let's say she's standing in rounds somewhere in the hospital. She often gets bored and so she uses that time to ground. While she's standing in rounds listening to nurses and physician's assistants talk about tests and treatments, meds, and the like, she sends her rope cord down to the center of the earth and imagines what it looks like down there, all the while she's right there in the nursing station. So, she's hooked in through the floors below her to the core of the earth. Rounds end, and she's still thinking about that cord as she walks around the hospital. Again, from a higher perspective, the little bit of distance she's moving from the center of the earth to around the hospital is negligible, if anything at all. However, from Kim's perspective, she feels like the cord is cutting through all the floors below her: hallways and people's offices, hospital rooms, disturbing the operating rooms. These are things her brain thinks about and struggles with.

We just wanted to share these thoughts that Kim has, so that when you have thoughts like this, or different ones all together, you will think of these examples and say, "I know if I explained this to Kim, she would get it."

Once you lay the foundation of getting into the wide-open space of anything is possible and you ground yourself deep in the core of the earth and lock in with Spirit or Highest Self above, this is when you start learning how to trust the messages you receive.

By now you've seen how essential it is to understand and manage your emotions to foster intuition. You now have tools to recognize where you are on the Polarity of Feelings line and methods to shift toward more positive emotions. As you continue this journey, remember that mastering your emotions is an ongoing practice, but one that builds the foundation for intuitive clarity. In the next chapter, we'll uncover "The Truth About Intuition" and how grounding yourself plays a pivotal role in receiving intuitive messages clearly and consistently. Stay tuned—you're about to step even deeper into the world of intuition!

Exercise 3: Meditation to Grow a Small Positive Feeling into Something Bigger

Begin by finding a comfortable seated position where you feel both safe and at ease. Start by breathing in and out at your natural rhythm, focusing on the sensation of your breath. Settle into a place of peace and relaxation. Allow your thoughts to come and go as they will—and please remember, though thoughts can evoke emotions, they are just thoughts.

Now, bring to mind a memory of something that felt really good. This could be the joy of a first date, the happiness of a family dinner filled with laughter, or the pride of receiving a well-deserved grade after studying hard. If you don't have a specific memory, imagine something that would make you feel amazing, such as winning a significant award or being recognized for an achievement you've always dreamed of.

Pay attention to where you feel this positive emotion in your body. Is it in your belly, your throat, or perhaps in your head? Notice how this excitement and joy manifests physically.

Science suggests that there is an energy field around you—often called by non-scientists an aura—extending about three feet from your body. Think of this aura as a bubble, like a soap bubble but with more substance. Feel this space around you, the bubble that represents your personal energy field.

Return to that good feeling you've identified. Immerse yourself in it completely. Visualize it as a golden, glittery light, a silvery shimmer, or any color that resonates with you, and imagine it filling your bubble. Let this light expand and grow, filling every part of your bubble, including your back, which can be challenging to reach.

As you fill your bubble with this light and good feeling, recognize that it started with a positive thought leading to a positive emotion. Now, seek to enhance this feeling further by reaching for even better thoughts, ones that elevate your mood even more.

If you encounter any resistance or sense a wall closing in, gently pull back. You might have pushed beyond your current capacity. Instead, focus on continuing to fill your bubble with the good feeling and gradually add other positive emotions like hope, joy, gratitude, and excitement.

Allow the feeling to rise and grow until you feel exuberant, hopeful, and as though the world is full of possibilities. Stay in this positive state for as long as you like. If you want to continue to expand your bubble or explore making it even larger, feel free to do so.

Thank you for letting us be part of this journey with you.

Exercise 4: Grounding Meditation

For this grounding meditation, I'm incorporating techniques from Jeffrey Allen's *Duality* program, Heather Alice Shea, and my mindfulness-based stress reduction training. This practice is designed to help you connect deeply with the earth, anchoring your energy in a way that supports your intuition and stability.

To begin, find a comfortable seated position, and if it feels right, go ahead and close your eyes. Allow your breath to become natural and focused. Simply feel the rhythm of your breath as it flows in and out, letting it guide you into a state of calm.

Now, allow yourself to become centered—whatever that means for you. If you're unsure how to do this, that's okay. This practice will help you discover what it feels like to be centered. One way to start is by bringing your attention to the top of your head, focusing on your brain space, and allowing a sense of centering to emerge.

When you're ready, I want you to imagine your root chakra. It's okay if this concept is new or unfamiliar—just go with it. Visualize that you have a root chakra, even if you're uncertain. Imagine it as a red energy center located at the base of your body, between your legs. This chakra is connected to feelings of safety, security, and being grounded. Take a moment to feel this energy center, noticing any sensations that arise. If the idea of focusing here feels uncomfortable, you can shift your awareness slightly higher, toward the area around your belly button, where the sacral chakra resides, glowing orange.

Next, I want you to imagine sending a thick, sturdy rope from your lower belly or root chakra down into the earth. Picture this rope as one of those heavy, multi-twined ropes used on ships in the 1800s—something that feels strong and unbreakable.

Visualize the rope descending from your body, through the floor, the foundation, and deep into the earth, all the way to its core. Take your time with this—let the rope extend further with each breath, grounding you more deeply with every moment.

As your rope reaches the earth's core, imagine what that place looks like. Perhaps you see stalagmites and stalactites, or maybe you sense warmth and flowing magma. Envision a space where you feel safe and grounded, a place that's uniquely yours. You might picture a cozy bedroom, a peaceful picnic spot, or a favorite beach spot—whatever feels right to you. Take a moment to stake your claim in this space, feeling the deep, core connection with the earth.

Pause here for a moment if you would like.

Once you feel rooted and secure, begin to follow the rope back up to your body, maintaining that strong connection with the earth. As you do, notice how your body feels. Are your legs heavier? Do your shoulders feel more relaxed? You might even experience a sense of sleepiness or a desire to yawn.

This deep grounding helps anchor your intuition in reality, providing a stable foundation as you listen to your inner guidance.

If you're sitting in a chair, imagine grounding all four legs into the earth. If you're on a meditation cushion, envision grounding all four corners of the perimeter of the space you take up in this sit into the earth as well. You can even extend this grounding to your home or office, picturing thick cords anchoring the four corners of your space deep into the earth. This grounding not only stabilizes you but can also create a sense of calm in your environment.

Finally, take a moment to feel the aliveness that comes from being deeply rooted in the earth. If you need more time in this grounded state, feel free to pause and stay here as long as you like. When you're ready, gently bring your awareness back to your surroundings, knowing that your connection with the earth remains strong and steady.

Thank you for allowing this meditation to be part of your practice.

Chapter Three

Truths About Intuition

In Chapter Three, we'll dive deep into the concept of intuition. You've probably heard people talk about their "gut feelings" or inner voice, but intuition is so much more than that. Intuition isn't just a mystical or magical phenomenon; it's a powerful, natural ability that every human possesses. It's the way your entire brain and body work together to gather subtle information from the world around you—sometimes even from sources beyond what we can see. All of this guides you toward making decisions that align with your highest good.

This chapter will explore what intuition is and isn't, how your body is involved in receiving these subtle signals, and how to trust what you're receiving. We'll break down some of the myths about intuition and help you understand that it's a skill you can develop and strengthen. Whether it's reading energy, interpreting signs from your surroundings, or simply following that quiet nudge inside, learning to trust your intuition can open the door to a more aligned, joyful life.

The specific tool you'll learn in this chapter is how to identify and dismantle the false beliefs you might hold about intuition, replacing them with empowering truths that will help you trust your inner guidance. By the end of this chapter, you'll be ready to begin unlocking your own intuitive abilities with confidence, and breaking free from doubt and misconceptions.

We want to remind you of the definition of intuition. Intuition is using your whole brain and body to receive all of the possible information available in order to make the best possible decision for your happiness. Your body is absolutely involved. Your body is the receiver, taking in information from the Field/the Vortex/whatever you want to call it. This is where the intuitive information comes from. There is information out in the ether ready for you; we are just teaching you how to tap in and access it.

Being grounded and rooted in both above and below is really important in order to maintain balance and perspective when you receive intuitive hits. The problem is that for so many people, when they receive words of intuition, they doubt what they are receiving. There is fear and myth that are a part of the belief system that make it hard to believe that what they are receiving is reality. Those doubts and beliefs need to be addressed.

There are a lot of false beliefs about intuition out there.

Here are just a few:

- **Intuition is just a gut feeling**. It's more than a gut feeling. It's your *whole brain and body receiving energy messages* that your brain processes as thoughts, images, lines from movies, and songs. We will get into this in later chapters.

- **Intuition is infallible**. Sometimes you read the energy wrong. Sometimes the energy changes. Sometimes it just doesn't work out the way you think it's going to. Heather Alice Shea says that your intuition is *never* wrong—the hit you get is correct; it's how you apply it, or interpret it that's sometimes "off" or "wrong."
- **Intuition is magical or mystical**. It's actually a skill set you can learn. Kim will show you how in later chapters.
- **Only certain people have intuition**. This one really bothers Kim. Let us say this very clearly. *Everyone is intuitive.* Everyone is walking in their intuition all the time. *Even you, dear reader!* Lee Harris says whenever anyone is really good at a particular task, their intuition is definitely involved.
- **Intuition and rationality are opposites**. No, one is right-brained and the other left-brained. One is a feeling, a "gut knowing" if you will, versus a head knowing. The two marry. You work the two of them together—your left and right brain working together.
- **Intuition is always conscious**. Nope. Most of what you do, according to Dr. Joe Dispenza, is done subconsciously. According to his book, *Breaking the Habit of Being Yourself,* 80% of our outward actions are based on your subconscious beliefs. When your intuition kicks in, it may have to bypass your subconscious and even your conscious to get you out of your rut. This kind of follows that rule for true/false quizzes—if you see the word "always," it can't be true.
- **Intuition is the same as instinct**. Your subconscious has one job: to keep you safe. That's it's job. If intuition were the same as instinct, "instinct" would also mean keeping you safe. And that is not the case; instinct means a fixed pattern of behavior in response to specific stimuli.

Sometimes we have instincts that will put us in grave danger. Intuition keeps us safe and tries to get us to not do something that is harmful. Intuition shows us the right way to go to save us time, money, and resources. It also tries to get us into situations that will present our best possible outcome, which can mean change and feelings of discomfort. Intuition opens the world of possibilities and adventure, which is not necessarily safe and might even go directly against our instincts.

- **Intuition is always clear and direct**. Oh, so far from it! We will talk about this at length in the coming chapters as well.
- **Intuition is all made up**. So many people think that intuition is fake or not something to value. Kim says for certain that she cannot live her life without her intuition. The internal guidance system is necessary to ensure that she is walking the path to her best possible future.

Please take a moment, dear reader, and think about what your beliefs are about intuition. Are they true? Do they light you up and excite you, or do they make you feel a little hopeless and sad? If they are a little hopeless and sad, they are probably lifeless, like the list up above.

But Kim doesn't like to stay in hopeless, sad, and lifeless feelings. She likes to focus on growth and change, but most of all HOPE. So, let's talk about beliefs about intuition that might light you up:

- **Intuition is a natural ability.** Trust me, it's inside of you. We will talk more about this after this list is over.
- **Intuition is a guide, not a guarantee**. Kim finds intuition to be a light in dark places. It gives her the hope that

everything is going to work out—no matter how her current reality looks. She might want what she wants, the way she wants it. Because Kim can't always read the energy for herself, having someone who can read the energy and tell her what they see encourages her beyond belief.

- **Intuition integrates experience and knowledge.** We talked about this up above a little with the right and left brain working together. This is the same concept. You integrate what you know about life, your experience, your desires, your knowledge, and it is married to your intuition. They are not separate. Your intuition uses your experience and knowledge to give you even greater insight.
- **Listening to intuition requires trust.** When Kim gets a particularly unbelievable hit with her intuition for herself, she reaches out to other intuitives in her life to get confirmation. This helps her trust that what she's hearing with her intuition is accurate. Even Kim struggles with trusting her intuition when it comes to hearing for herself.
- **Intuition complements rational thought.** Again, this is your left and right brain working together. Intuition can enhance rational decision-making, providing a holistic approach to problem-solving.
- **Intuition often comes as subtle whispers.** Do you know how many times Kim's intuition tried to get her to listen, and because it can be swatted away like a fly, she just ignored it? More often than not, your intuition is a soft, kind, gentle voice or nudge. It requires attention, that's for sure. It also takes some insight and discernment.
- **Embracing intuition enhances personal growth.** Because your intuition takes you out of your current understandings and ruts, following it can take you out of your natural ways

of doing things—from the way you grocery shop, to the way you drive to work one day. It might not always make sense why you are being asked to turn from normal ways of doing things, but your intuition asks you go differently to bring new things into your life and to build trust.

- **Intuition is an inner compass.** Melanie Warner from My Defining Moments states that 80% of people in the world never find their purpose or calling. *This is the heart of why Kim is writing this book.* We ask our 18-year-olds to decide what the rest of their lives are going to look like. But what if you decided wrong and life is now feeling flat? Your intuition can help you move yourself out of the flatness to create hope and joy.
- **Courage is key to following intuition.** Do you know how many times Kim's intuition has told her to go talk to someone, step out of her comfort zone, asks her to say YES! to an unknown experience? Every time she steps out in trust, she builds trust with her intuition. Kim also looks at her experiences as learning moments—even if they were challenging, or even down-right unenjoyable. It takes that first step of hearing, and then lifting up your foot and stepping into right action, as guided by your intuition.
- **When you know how, hearing your intuition is easy.** Kim found a mentor for herself. She gives readings for others and encourages them to trust what they are sensing. She leads groups of people to hear, and trust, and know what their intuition is saying. Because hearing your intuition doesn't just give insight into *every* situation, it also changes your circumstances.
- **Intuition is just a muscle.** You can learn how to strengthen it.

– **Intuition is absolutely real.** Lots of people think intuition is made up or stuff of the imagination. The "problem" with intuition is you need to learn to discern which "voice" of your thoughts is your ego/left brain and which is your intuition. That is the biggest learning curve. When you figure that out, you and your intuition are working together.

Intuition is a natural ability.

Ever go to an auto mechanic who speaks to cars? All of a sudden, they poke their head out from under the hood and make an announcement about a heat shield, alternator, camshaft, axle, or some other car part—like a line or a plug and it's just something they know?

Other examples are the Dog Whisperer.

The Horse Whisperer.

Did you ever bump into somebody who just knew how to look at accounting books and like the numbers all lined up and it just all clicked and it all made sense to them? They just knew what they knew.

Einstein knew E equals MC squared before he could prove it. He knew it. He knew it and he said, "This is truth," before they could prove it.

When you are involved in some aspect of creativity and flow and it just all comes alive for you, that is your intuition. When you are able to do something that other people just aren't able to do and you think it's completely normal and natural for you, your intuition is guiding you. When you are confused by somebody else who can't do what is normal and natural for you, your intuition is guiding you.

Take Tom Brady and quarterbacking or Travis Kelce rescripting what a tight end does all together. Actually, let's talk about Travis Kelce for a moment. His ability to read a field, know where the ball is going to be, and read where he has to put his body? All of that is intuition.

Everybody has that gift in some area. There are times when Kim is knitting that other people are just like, "How are you doing that?" and she says, "I don't know. It all just makes sense to me." But she has to follow a pattern. She says she can't write a knitting pattern to save her life or create a hat out of nothing. She has a friend who will just pick up yarn and she will start knitting hats and just know what she's doing intuitively. No written pattern and the pattern is all in her head with bobbles and cables. She just feels her way through it.

Wherever you see somebody walking in gifts that seem supernatural and don't make sense completely to you but they are able to create miracles and move mountains in their field, they are walking in their intuition. I might appear to be miraculous or magical—it just appears that way because intuition is a flow state, an accessing of alternate information. To those who don't understand, intuition appears to be supernatural.

Intuition is absolutely real.

Einstein says we absolutely have to be using our imagination in order to create a future that is exciting and wonderful. Yes, that is your imagination, but it is also your intuition. It is your intuition creating a fantasy that turns into reality when you dream it into being.

When Kim was in college, she was asked to complete a journal on a 12-day backpacking experience and as a part of that journal entry, she made a list of things she wanted to do in her future that seemed impossible at the time. She had no recollection that she had even made this list when she found it about a decade later. One of the items on this list was to knit a sweater. When she found this list, she had just finished knitting her first sweater. If she hadn't had the dream of knitting a sweater a decade before, would she have seeded the inspiration to create one?

When you get an intuitive hit, it might feel a little like an imagination or "an undigested bit of beef, a blot of mustard, a crumb of cheese, or a fragment of underdone potato," as Ebenezer Scrooge says of Marley when he shows up in *A Christmas Carol*. The truth is, your intuition is valid and real. It is a true source of guidance in your life. To ignore it is to ignore that you have two legs or two arms. Everybody knows the value of their limbs and their digits to be able to walk and maneuver in this lifetime, whether you have full use of them or not. Cutting off your intuition and the knowledge that it brings limits you just as much as losing a limb or a digit would limit your abilities to perform, maneuver, and create.

Intuition is logical and rational but comes from the right hemisphere of your brain.

Most people live in the left hemisphere of their brains. Most people are only paying attention to their logic, their ego, and the trappings of the subconscious. When the right hemisphere is engaged, more artistic, free-flowing, feeling experiences take shape. For the extremely logical of the world, it is challenging to allow space for the ideas that originate in the right-hemisphere or in the body. The left-brained are focused on logic, reason, and thoughts of the ego. Anything that originates outside of that is uncomfortable and, often, shut down quickly.

We're asking Kim to tell a story that makes her really vulnerable, open, and exposed. We ask for your patience as she does this. It is not an easy story to tell.

There was a time in my life when I was a hardcore Christian who had a fundamentalist stick up my butt. I was judgy, condemning, and expected perfection from myself and from those around me. I had forgotten the grace given to me and that I was to give grace to others. Though I wasn't very graceful with those around me, I expected everyone to give me all the grace for any flaws I may have had. It was a weird time in my 20s and even my 30s, is all I can say of it now.

Here and now, in the writing of these words, I want to be very clear. Wherever I am in my faith and wherever I am in my spiritual walk, I have nothing but respect for the Holy Spirit and will never ever disrespect the Holy Spirit. Ever. I am very careful of how I maneuver around the Godhead in terms of the Holy Spirit. When I stepped away from faith and God, I stepped out of intuition for years. I first found my intuition in the Holy Spirit and if I wasn't honoring the Godhead, then I wasn't going to hear my intuition. It felt disrespectful to the Holy Spirit.

I now have permission from Spirit to walk in intuition and teach it. I received that permission on a seven-day silent retreat I attended at Omega Institute in Rhinebeck, New York, while I was studying to be a qualified Mindfulness-Based Stress Reduction instructor.

So, as I tell this story, please know I am grateful for my history but I am also grateful for how much I have grown.

There was a time in my early 20s, I went out to Paradise, California and stayed with my best friend from college and her family. While I was at their house, my best friend's mom gave me a book to read by Benny Hinn and I devoured it. I have always been a spirit junkie. I have always been looking to feel more and be more in this lifetime. I was looking for Spirit to fill me with passion and meaning. I was looking for that good feeling high that Spirit is able to give. Benny Hinn's book opened so many experiences of how to feel and see the Holy Spirit.

After I got back home to the North Shore of Boston after the visit to California, I wanted more Spirit in my life. I would drive around Cape Ann on all the little back roads by the ocean, trying to figure out how to speak in tongues. Benny Hinn and his book said that the gifts of the Holy Spirit are for today and therefore you should be able to access them. My very strong left hemisphere brain really struggled with how to just turn off thoughts and allow sounds to come out of my mouth. How was that even possible? So, I would drive around with the radio off or with Christian music playing very loud. I would "prime the pump" for the gift of tongues, and hum or drop my jaw and say, "Ah," in the hopes of getting it to just come out. I had no idea what to do, or how to do it.

The only guidance my best friend's mom gave me was, "Just open your mouth and start making the sounds."

I looked at her and said, "How do you do that?"

She said, "You just do."

I would find myself with the feeling of Spirit inside my chest rising up. I realize this might sound like a bizarre statement. It felt like a pressure and fullness. Not in a bad way, but in a peaceful overflowing love way. Once the feeling was in my chest, I would try really hard to get that feeling out of my mouth in the form of tongues. Only, it wouldn't come out. It just wouldn't. I was blocking its flow by thinking too much or trying too hard. I would be putting pressure on it and cut it off from happening.

Anytime I would relax enough and start to feel the buildup of Spirit in my chest, the feeling would start a hum in the back of my throat, and it would make me start to feel the words forming in the back of my mouth. I would get so excited. I would pull my thoughts out of the feeling and I would think, "OH! What am I going to say?"

This was my left brain taking over. This was my ego looking for control.

It would shut down all the feelings that had built up in my chest. The feeling bubble would pop and nothing would come of it. I would deflate like a balloon and there was nothing to come out of my mouth. The intensity in my chest would drop off and I would have to start all over.

It was literally six months to a year of me just making random noises while alone in my car, driving around aimlessly, in the hopes that my right brain would take over and just start talking. It did happen, eventually. Mostly because I didn't give up. I made it a priority and a mission to get my mouth to work without my brain engaged in analyzing and overthinking the words coming out. It took practice and the willingness to feel and look a bit foolish.

It wasn't until I started to work with my mentor years later at The Barn in Landenberg, Pennsylvania that I began to realize that intuitive words are just like speaking in tongues. You just open your mouth and trust that what you are about to say comes from Source. You trust that what is coming out is for the highest good and the edification of those who are receiving the intuitive hits.

Heather Alice Shea in her *True Intuition* work points out that science is proving intuition regularly. They can measure your energetic field. They can even see it.

Science is now proving what others have known for years. People have been calling it an aura for centuries—ancient Egypt made reference to it, but didn't call it that. But now that science can newly confirm they can measure the energy field around you, it's real.

Energy is all around us and it's in everything, which is fifth grade science.

People who are near each other share their energy field with each other.

When you are tapped into the Vortex, you are in that energy field. In fact, Dr. Joseph Dispenza, calls the Vortex, "The Field," for that very reason. We are all tapping into the same energy space.

Want to know how The Field is real? There are those stories of twins or family members who aren't near each other, but know when something bad has happened to their loved one from one side of the world to the other. They don't have to be in close proximity to know that something bad has occurred with someone they care about deeply. Lisa Beamer in her book *Let's Roll*, tells the story of her experiences on 9/11/2001. She wrote in her book that she heard about the planes, the issues, and knew that she knew her husband was on one of them. She didn't have proof, but her body collapsed, bringing her to the floor, while she was five months pregnant. Her brain learned later what her body knew, Lisa Beamer's husband was on the flight that crashed in Pennsylvania, but was on the way to the Pentagon.

This is the energy field we are all in. Once you step into this field, information is just available to you. Once you know how to tap in and access it, all the information in The Field is available to you. Everybody accesses this information in different ways and learning the way that you access this information is essential for you to be able to trust your intuition.

Intuition is normal.

You don't have to be a guru or a meditator or a yoga instructor or some sort of spiritual teacher in order to be able to tap into your intuition. Everyone has the ability to be intuitive. Everybody's body is poised and set to receive information from the Universe for the betterment of the whole. Whether that is in trade, as stated above when a mechanic is a Car Whisperer, or whether that is in art where authors just have stories flow out of them. Everybody has the potential to tap into their intuition to create hope and joy and excitement for those around them, no matter their faith and no matter their training. Often, however, where you have aptitude and skills, that is where your intuition shines out.

Kim took a course about how to hear God with a man named John Paul Jackson, who was a prophet in New Hampshire. He said in this course that one time he went to a festival or a fair that had a whole bunch of psychics lined up in stalls. They were being paid to give people readings. He said he wanted to be like Jesus in the temple when Jesus was turning over the tables of the money lenders because the money lenders were desecrating the house of God with materialistic practices, fleecing the people. John Paul Jackson felt these psychics were frauds because they weren't his truth—they weren't of God. Only John Paul Jackson stated that as he was walking around, the Holy Spirit started to show him that one person didn't have a real gift, but that a different person, though they weren't in Christ, did have a real gift given by God. John Paul Jackson stated his paradigm was blown and he was shaken. He was bothered that some people who didn't even know God and weren't in the Christian Godhead would have gifts from the Father, Son, and Holy Spirit.

What this story embodies for Kim is that everyone at that psychic event was able to use their intuition to help others. What it also shows is that people—no matter their faith background, their life experiences, their place in life—are able to tap into the field where intuition resides and help others.

Everybody has gifts. Everybody has something they are really good at. Where you excel is where the door to intuition opens for you. What you are able to do well and with ease, that is the area where you are walking in your intuition, even if you don't see it.

Kim has a couple of best friends. One of them built an ice-skating rink in her backyard, a small one for her children when they were little. Kim's friend built it out of boards and plastic and water that froze over in her backyard in Massachusetts during the winter. The friend would put her little children (think aged two or three) in snowsuits that made their arms bounce and cushioned their little bodies. The kids would wear little tiny skates and the friend just pushed them out onto the ice. The older of the two girls started to do all sorts of turns and jumps. She started to dance on the ice. She allowed her body to take over and she allowed the flow of skating to lead the way. This led Kim's best-friend to sign this daughter up for skating lessons at a very young age. Now, she is a professional figure skater and is establishing herself as a figure skating coach.

Interestingly enough, Kim's best friend's younger daughter is an ice hockey player and plays on a competitive travel team as well as playing varsity on her female hockey team for her high school, as a freshman.

Both of these girls have taken their experiences at a young age with a homemade ice-skating rink in the backyard, created skills, and continue to allow their intuition to guide them on the ice in each of their practices. Young people need experiences and opportunities to grow their own passions. This is why the arts in schools and exposure to theater and music and all kinds of experiences really matter for everybody, because until you are exposed to these things, you won't know what lights you up and what makes you shine. You may not know what areas your intuition will just flow out naturally and with ease.

When you come to accept that intuition is real, normal, and an experience that everyone has, it allows you the opportunity to explore the ways that your intuition speaks to you the most.

Knowing how hard it can be to trust what you are hearing and experiencing with your intuition, we challenge you to find two or three of these truths that you find particularly powerful and meaningful. Write them on an index card, on a sticky note, in your planner every week. Put them in places where you will see them regularly (think your car's dashboard, your bathroom mirror, on the milk in the refrigerator), so that you help yourself to remember the truths about intuition so they become beliefs. As Esther Hicks says, "A belief is a thought you keep thinking." Allow these truths to become foundational beliefs for you. Think about them regularly. Allow them to shape what they mean for you.

Now that we've peeled back the layers of what intuition truly is—and isn't—you should feel a little lighter, perhaps more hopeful about your own intuitive potential. Remember, intuition is not reserved for a select few; it's inside all of us, waiting to be embraced. You now understand that your intuition is a partner, working in tandem with your rational mind to help you navigate life's complexities.

In the next chapter, we'll explore how to deepen your connection with this powerful tool by learning how to enter

Chapter Three

into your intuition intentionally. You'll discover techniques for grounding, quieting the mind, and tuning into the subtle whispers of your inner guidance. This is where you begin to step into the flow and make decisions with clarity and confidence. Let's embark on this next step of the journey together!

Chapter Four

How to Enter into Your Intuition

Imagine standing at a crossroads, unsure which path to take. Now, picture having a calm inner voice guiding you—one that knows exactly which turn leads to your greatest joy, success, and fulfillment. This chapter will teach you how to access that voice, your intuition, and how to trust its quiet wisdom. As you become attuned to it, you'll find decisions—whether in business, relationships, or personal growth—becoming easier and more aligned with your true self.

The specific tool we'll focus on here is *using your learning style to learn how your intuition speaks to you most clearly*. This means learning how to recognize and distinguish between your ego's loud, frantic "voice" and your intuition's calm, sure guidance. You'll begin by exploring how intuition feels, how it communicates, and how you can create a space in your life to strengthen this connection.

By the end of this chapter, you'll understand the various ways intuition speaks—whether through metaphors, physical sensations, visuals, or thoughts—and be ready to integrate this inner wisdom into your daily life. You'll also see how intuition can save you time and help you make decisions with clarity and confidence, as it has for many others.

When your intuition begins to speak to you and you know what you are hearing and listening to, it will open doors in your life that were not available when the doors of intuition were closed.

Your intuition will help you be a better business person and it will help you make decisions you weren't able to make quickly before. You will know what is right and what is wrong. Those decisions of turning left or right at a crossroads or at a fork in the road of your life will be so much easier because you will know how to hear from your inner voice and your inner wisdom. You will be able to experience certainty in the midst of what you cannot figure out logically. You will feel sure about decisions you are making knowing that you are headed towards your best possible future, that you are headed towards happiness, that you are headed towards feeling better than you feel right now. Your intuition helps you make these decisions and helps you know the path.

Cristina Leeson, author of *Live in the Light, Respect the Dark,* says following your intuition saves you time, money, and aggravation.

For a long time, Kim struggled with how to hear. She was working really hard to hear Spirit. She wanted to know Spirit and so she thought she was listening for voices. So, she would be looking at all of the thoughts inside her head and sometimes those thoughts would be her intuition leading her correctly and sometimes those thoughts would be muddled and her own ego.

It took her a long, long time to be able to decipher her own ego's loud thoughts versus her intuition's calm knowing thoughts.

Sometimes we would say "turn left" and she would go left and then she would meet the boy she liked. One time, when Kim was in her early 20s, we even told her to park her car outside of his dorm room. She had no idea where she was going. She had never been there before. We got her there, up a stairwell, down a different stairwell, through a corridor, and around another corridor, past a bunch of guys tossing a football in the middle of a hallway, to this man's closed door. She knocked and she had no idea what she was going to say when he opened the door. She had no idea why she was even there. She just knew she was being directed.

We protected her. He was not there. No one was there.

She was so confused at the time. However, we wanted to show her what it felt like to decide to move by intuition. We used something that she was deeply invested in, this guy.

He wasn't the right guy for her. We knew that.

We had him away when she showed up. Intentionally. But we needed her to be vested in the process of learning and, as a result, she listened carefully to each of our directions—left, right, upstairs, downstairs. We got her there. She knew she was led and it helped her to hear our voice better.

However, we didn't want her to meet the guy, because he was not her guy.

We will use whatever we need to use to get you to where you need to be with your intuition. That may appear to be a painful experience in that what you want isn't being delivered. But we use the thing that you want to get you there. But you are human, a lovely, beautiful, wonderful human and we have nothing but love and power and grace for you. You are powerful and your ability to create is powerful. We want to help you create the best possible life for yourself.

In that wandering the hallways of a seminary moment in Kim's life we were directing her, yes. We were trying to teach her and she was an active learner. We gave her direct statements in the form of directions in those moments—left, right, up, down, but she was pressing in to hear. That was what she wanted. She wanted to hear.

We don't always work with thoughts. To be honest, it is one of the harder ways to work with intuition. Trying to parse and discern if your thought is your thought or our thought? To be honest, if you aren't an auditory learner (which Kim isn't), that has the potential to be a difficult way to learn intuition.

Without knowing it, to be honest, Kim chose one of the hardest ways to learn intuition *for her*. She was focused on hearing. However, Kim's strengths are not listening. Kim is better with metaphor. Whenever Kim gives a talk, she centers her illustrations around using metaphor as the foundation of the story. When she talks about getting visions and signs and downloads for people, very often those come in metaphor. She sees visions of things like when she's reading a book in her head and she's no longer in the room but she's living inside of a mini-movie we are showing to her. Kim's imagination is visual and active.

We use that.

One night at a retreat center in the Poconos of Pennsylvania, Kim was having a conversation with a man who had recently lost his wife and was discussing how much he loved being alone. He was grieving the loss of her, yes, but he was also excited to have space to himself. As Kim was talking to him, she saw a swimming pool in her head. It was fall at the time of the conversation and there wasn't a swimming pool at the retreat center. As far as Kim could tell, the swimming pool in her imagination seemed like a weird fit. There was not a reason that she could see for having the visual of a swimming pool inside her head in the middle of this conversation about grief and freedom, so she sat with the swimming pool. She waited for the swimming pool to make sense. She didn't rush it. She didn't push at it. She just said, "Why am I seeing a swimming pool?" and then she waited.

What eventually arose was the image of pruney fingers when one has been in water too long. She realized that this man she was talking to was swimming around in feeling good in his solitude. He was enjoying his solitude and he was content. But, the pruney fingers gave Kim insight. Kim said, "There may come a time when that solitude no longer feels good. Being in a swimming pool feels good until it doesn't. When your fingers get pruney and your body gets tired of being in the water, it's time to come out. When it doesn't feel good anymore."

Kim said, "There may come a time when you feel like solitude is no longer contentment and satisfying. It may turn into loneliness and longing." She said, "There's nothing wrong with that. Be where you are and notice when and if that starts to shift."

A swimming pool by itself does not always mean discontentment with one's life. In fact, a swimming pool often connotes joy and exuberance and satisfaction and success. In this instance, however, Kim had to wait for the swimming pool to reveal its meaning.

Visual images from your intuition are applicable in so many areas of life. Think about businesses and places of work where people need to decide about selling and buying stocks, or to sign a contract or not, or to bring in that particular client or not, or to move forward with a house renovation or not. The answers may come in as hard yes'es and no's if you know how to listen to them. However, big life decisions don't always come in that way. Sometimes you get a visual inside your head. Or you get a song lyric in your head that just happens to answer your question. Or you get an emotional charge or an emotional sense that something will be a good thing or a bad thing.

Laura Day, in her book *How to Rule the World from Your Couch*, tells the story of a man using his intuition to watch stocks and companies. He was interested in a company that was somehow attached to agriculture—maybe it was a seed company or a fertilizer company. The logo for the company was a bunny rabbit. He said that once he learned to trust his intuition, he would sit in his office every morning and give his intuition time to make notes and he would take them down. One morning, he saw a bunny rabbit on skis going downhill. Then he saw the bunny rabbit get on a chairlift. Once the rabbit was on top of the hill again, he watched the bunny go back down the hill again. Then he watched the bunny go back up the chairlift again and this time, the bunny went up higher and stayed up. At first, he was stumped by the bunny and the visual, until he connected the visual he saw in his imagination to the company with the rabbit logo. He said that the company's stocks dropped. He knew that the stocks would drop and then rise and then drop according to the number of times he watched the bunny slide down the hill.

How do you start creating a space where visuals are welcome? Where ideas are welcome?

Let's give another example. Kim has a good friend who is learning to trust her intuition. One of the things she does to support her learning is she uses her strengths. She knows her body is really strong at picking up empathy and other people's emotions. She is someone who works with people to help them create their full potential in their lives. She is extremely talented at being able to read other people's emotions and other people's feelings. When talking with Kim, this friend is able to pick up Kim's feelings and say, "I feel the pressure of that in my chest. It's really deep and heavy. It also makes my throat tight." What she said she felt were the exact same feelings Kim was experiencing in her body.

Kim likes to say that learning to be empathetic is dipping your toes in the waters of intuition. If you want to start to learn how to be intuitive, an easy way to do that is through empathy. Kim also says that empathy is the most accepted version of intuition in most institutions at this point of history. Managers are expected to "read the room" and the expression, "read the room," means to know how people are feeling before you even say a word. Managers, supervisors, and colleagues are expected to know how what they are saying is being received without hearing any verbal feedback. They are expected to be able to *feel* the emotional feedback.

Reading the room is an open, expected, accepted skill that is based on empathy and empathy is the door to deeper intuition.

Cristina Leeson says that the guides talk to you in your head using your voice and it's your first, immediate thoughts that are your intuition. Your ego comes in after, and argues with you. She says the ego is the second voice, it's loud, argumentative, and wants attention. Your ego stops you from doing anything new, scary, or out of the box. Because your ego loves control, it will do all it can to stop you, to keep you small and safe. If you are able to tell the difference between your ego shouting and the still, small, quiet, voice of your intuition, you'll be able to be guided by your intuition. She says that the body is an instrument that can feel other people's emotions and be able to read the room. She says you get visions, daydreams, deja vu's, and aha moments and those are your intuition. She says "You can hear stuff, like a stop, or a go," and sometimes you just know in your bones. Signs are validation that you're hearing it right along the way.

There are tools that can guide you into your intuition.

As an educator, Kim was expected to help people learn using their learning styles. To be honest when Kim first found out that she was a kinesthetic learner, she was annoyed. She thought it was an annoying learning style. It's not traditional like visual or auditory learners. The good thing about being a kinesthetic learner is that you learn through doing. You have somebody explain it, show it to you, and then you immediately want to dive in and be the one to do it yourself.

Auditory learners take information by listening. They're the kind of people who would always have music playing.

Visual learners are the kind of people who will gravitate toward movies and will gravitate toward things they see—most often objects and how objects can be metaphors for situations in their own lives.

Kim is kinesthetic—she learns through doing. However, she is also visual. This means that she gets images and ideas as a picture inside her head. She has to translate that image to her listener, so Kim often talks in metaphor. Yes, she can still have her intuition use an auditory experience for guidance. She has had that occasion where she was asking the big existential life question—she turned on her car and the music lyric blaring at that moment gave her a direct answer she needed to hear in that moment.

According to Heather Alice Shea, if you know your learning style, you know the best way to enter into your intuitive style. They go hand-in-hand. If you don't know your learning style, you could google learning style and take a test online. Basically, the visual learners will get images in their head. The auditory learners will hear either inside their head or outside their head or they'll get music lyrics through their head or they'll get something like a line their dad used to say all the time as a response to somebody's question. The kinesthetic learner has it rough and we want Kim to tell this story.

It was the first time I had been at a training at my then church. I didn't know the instructor or really anybody there. It was a training to help us step into our intuition. The instructor told me to go up and just tell somebody something.

I had all sorts of fears about this:

– What if I was wrong?
– What if I didn't get anything?
– What if I said something stupid?

I addressed these to the man leading the class and he laughed. He said, "Go. Do it."

The "what if's" continued to play in my head.

So, I went up to this woman who I didn't know.

I stood in front of her and my mind was completely blank.

Nothing was coming in. She was looking at me expectantly and I had nothing.

I didn't know her at all. I had never met her before.

For all the kinesthetics out there, your intuition comes in one of two ways. The first way is a deep knowing in your gut and the second way is that you just open your mouth and give whatever pops out of your mouth. The second way is scarier, because sometimes, you have no idea what you are going to say when you start speaking.

Facing this woman, I had nothing.

Silence.

That's what I had.

Total silence.

Nothing like being on the spot.

Looking back, I could have taken a page out of Cristina Leeson's book. I met her years later and she said, "When you get nothing, just make it up. Let your imagination go, and make up the story." This is an especially good practice when working with Oracle cards.

So, here I was, standing in front of this woman, with a completely blank mind. It felt like forever, and I had nothing to say.

She was sitting in her chair. She looked up at me and she sort of had this little smile on her face that I took as being smug, because I didn't know her very well.

I fumbled around and eventually, I said, "You're not reading your Bible as much as you used to."

And she got offended. She was defensive when she said, "I am too reading my Bible. I sit and read my Bible like I do every morning. I meet with God. I have stopped reading for breadth and now I read for depth. I am taking it verse by verse and I'm chewing on it."

She explained she was taking the teachings of Paul very seriously. She said she was chewing on the verses more slowly, rather than reading large chunks of the Bible quickly—as one tends to when trying to read the whole Bible in one year.

I walked away feeling small. I felt I got it wrong because she said I was wrong.

As a brand new intuitive, I picked up that there was a change in her Bible reading habits. What I actually said was, "You're not reading your Bible as much as you used to," which she may have taken to be judgey. I didn't mean it as a judgment—it was the only thing that came into my head!

Chapter Four

I went back to the instructor, a man who became my mentor over the years, and I was like, "I totally messed it up. I flubbed it. I have no idea what I'm doing."

He asked, "Well, what happened?"

I told him, "I told her she wasn't reading her Bible as much as she used to. And then she said that she's reading for depth instead of breadth and blah, blah, blah. Now, I got it wrong, because she is like taking the verses slow."

He looked down at me and started this deep belly laugh that I came to adore.

"Kim," he said, "you totally got it right! You picked it up. You heard what was happening. She hasn't been reading as much of her Bible as she used to. She isn't; she slowed down. You heard correctly! She just didn't receive it very well!"

Now, dear reader, back to you. How are you going to receive and hear and listen and give yourself space and time to know, to tap in, to ground, and to connect with Source? How are you going to explore the training ground that is your intuition? That's the first question we would like you to answer. Are you going to take 10 minutes before your work day, like the man who saw what the bunny does? Are you going to be open to it as it flies in, as Kim is? Are you going to have a dedicated morning sit as Kim does?

We have another strategy we want to share. This one is for those of you out there who love a good journaling session. It will change the way you journal forever. It is this concept that we want to explore in the next chapter—how do you use writing to help you hear your intuition? This is a practice that Kim engages in regularly and she finds so much comfort in it, most of the time.

You've taken the first steps into the world of intuition, learning to tune in and discern its subtle yet powerful messages. Whether through a flash of imagery, a quiet knowing, or a physical nudge, your intuition is now a trusted guide, ready to help you navigate life's decisions with ease. As you continue on this journey, you'll notice that intuition often speaks in unexpected ways, sometimes through writing. In the next chapter, we'll explore *automatic writing*—a tool that can deepen your connection to your inner wisdom and provide new insights. Ready to pick up the pen? Let's dive in!

Chapter Five
Asking for Signs and Automatic Writing

Welcome to Chapter Five, where we dive into the powerful practice of automatic writing—a tool that allows you to receive guidance from Source directly onto paper. This is a sacred communication between your conscious self and higher energies. The process is simple: you pose a question, such as, "What do I need to know today?" or "How do I invite more abundance into my life?" Then, through a meditative state, you let the words flow, trusting that what comes is wisdom from beyond. Automatic writing can be as insightful as it is grounding, offering clarity on life's pressing questions or simply the reassurance that you're on the right path.

    What makes this practice even more fascinating is the diversity of energies you can connect with—whether it's your Higher Self, spirit guides, or even specific archetypes like Archangel Michael or Joan of Arc. Each brings its own tone and insight. This chapter will teach you how to begin automatic writing and explore the richness of this practice, leading you to greater peace, guidance, and self-understanding.

The practice that Kim calls automatic writing was first introduced to her by John Paul Jackson in that CD course she took from him years ago.

The idea of it is simple. Write down a question, tap into Source, and then write the response.

The questions you ask can be as simple as, "What do I need to know for today?"

"Is there something I'm overlooking?"

"What does Source want me to know overall?"

You can also ask questions like, "What will make me happy?"

"How do I improve my current living situation?"

"How do I make more money?"

You can explore different sources. This is where you find that different energy sources have different tones and styles.

Kim often taps into her Higher Self and we always just love telling her how great she is and how wonderful she is and how everything is always going to work out. Because we are always so positive, she gets frustrated with us. She has taken breaks from automatic writing throughout the years, because we tell her things that make her feel good. That feeling doesn't always line up with what she sees in the physical, and so, at times, she thinks we aren't to be trusted.

At times, we want her to be encouraged.

She asks almost impossible to answer questions—will he be around or will I marry him?

The truth is: Yes, she will marry A him, but it may not be THE him she means.

But the answer is yes.

Kim has a hard time believing all of this "she will get married one day" talk because Kim is 48 at the time of this being published and she's still unmarried. She feels that we're lying. Or worse, that

Chapter Five

the Universe is letting her down. Our goal is to encourage her to not give up hope. Her response is to think, "Hope is a fickle bitch," and move forward with making bigger and bigger plans for her life.

We think this is an important time to tell the story of a number of years ago.

Kim was talking to a friend of hers, who is an intuitive and uses The Guides as her Source. At this moment in Kim's life, she really, really wanted this job as a therapist at a boarding school. It would have been an on-campus position, the kind of job that would have consumed her time. It would have been a bit of a distance from where she lives now, like an hour or an hour and a half away.

As Kim was speaking to her friend, the friend suggested Kim ask the Guides for a sign that she was going to get the job. The friend said to put 24 hours on it so the Guides had a timeframe to work in.

Kim asked to see a caterpillar and a snail, because she felt it would be a challenging request. The friend reminded her that they could come as a balloon in the hospital, or an illustration on the side of a truck, a song lyric, or a topic of discussion in the nursing station, not just an actual snail or caterpillar.

Walking home from the hospital that day, she saw a black and brown caterpillar climbing up a fence post on a split rail fence as she came down the hill over the railroad tracks.

She then went out to dinner and was still waiting for the snail. She came home from dinner and swore there was no way she was going to find a snail in her apartment. She swore she knew her apartment, and felt nothing but disappointment. She railed at us, the Guides, Spirit, Source (use the words you want), because she felt that there wasn't a snail in her living space and she was disappointed that the job wouldn't be hers.

Kim was up and pacing. We directed her to her bedroom. In the dark. We moved her to the bookcase in her room, and we guided her to lift her hand—still in the dark. She didn't have a clue what she was raising her hand to, until she picked up a tiny, forgotten figurine of a snail that she had bought in the Czech Republic years and years before.

She had her snail.

She had her caterpillar.

That was the only summer she grew tomatoes. Every morning, she went out and watered the tomatoes and every morning as she moved the hose, she found snails hanging out under the cool protection of the hose.

She took all of this to mean she was going to get the job.

On the job interview, she had been informed that she would be called in a couple of days to be told if she had the position, because the person who was making the decision wanted to go on vacation and wanted to get this decided before she left. When Kim didn't hear anything before the vacation was set to start, Kim assumed that she would hear at some point…. Hopefully…. And then, eventually….

Maybe a month and a half later, Kim called to follow up on the job and left a voicemail. Kim received a call back about the job while she was out with friends at a high tea on a Saturday afternoon. Kim was informed, "It was a challenging decision," and "Everyone was impressed with her," but they had given the job to someone else. Kim just knew that the job was supposed to be hers, but they had given it to someone who had pull with the board, or had some sort of connection to the school, which Kim did not.

Chapter Five

To say that Kim was disappointed would be an understatement. Like we said, she really wanted this job.

Something else about Kim? She doesn't ask for signs anymore. Never to rarely.

When she does ask for them and we reply, she doesn't believe them. Which leads her to think, "What's the point?"

But this is not where the story of the boarding school therapist job ends.

She didn't get the job.

Then a few months later, in what would have been the start of the new job and the fall of the school year, her father got very sick. In fact, he died the day before Thanksgiving that year. From late August when the job would have kicked off in earnest to Thanksgiving, Kim spent most of her time in the evenings and on the weekends in his hospital room or at his room in the short-term rehab.

She made the phone calls, asked for tests and test results, and asked a lot of questions.

If she had been at the job she really wanted, she wouldn't have been able to be there for him the way that she was. It would have been an all-consuming job with little time to be there for her father.

That was 2019.

In 2021, on her birthday she called her favorite psychic and asked for an update on her life. Kim was on vacation at the beach in Cape May, New Jersey, sitting on the bed in a bed and breakfast, a block from the water.

The psychic told her that she would be offered a contract job and that Kim would take it. The contract would be for a year, and that Kim wasn't to worry about what would happen after the contract ended. Kim still felt nervous about what would happen after the contract was over and if she should accept this theoretical contract position. Kim also couldn't understand how she was going to be offered a contract position.

Kim spoke to the psychic the day before her birthday, maybe even directly on her birthday that year.

A week later, on a Monday, she was back from vacation and she was at work doing her job, standing in the infant ICU, attending rounds. During rounds, Kim received a text about a contract job at a school. It was the same kind of job that she would have been doing at the boarding school, only this role was for a therapist at a local, public middle school / high school.

The caterpillar and the snail showed her she would get a school therapist position. Only it wasn't the job she was craving. It was two years later, when the timing was better for her family's needs, and in a position that was in a location where she could still be close to her mom. She got the job she wanted, two years later, and it turned out to be one of her favorite jobs ever.

Sometimes when doing automatic writing, what you hear and what you see don't line up. That can be discouraging and that's what bothers Kim about it. It doesn't stop her from doing it. She has learned that what she's hearing may not be exactly what she's going to see when it all pans out, that what she's asking and what we're agreeing to are not actually the same things. This frustrates her and then she takes a break from automatic writing.

To be honest, automatic writing is a technique that makes her feel more peaceful—that and meditation.

For automatic writing, she grounds down and she taps in above to her highest self.

She asks big life questions, often about the things that are hurting her emotional heart. She asks questions about life, and love, about happiness, and joy. She knows that she feels better when she is tapped into Source, hearing words of encouragement and love from us.

What she finds kind of funny is that when she taps into Archangel Michael rather than her Highest Self, Archangel Michael is blunt, straightforward, not impolite but not necessarily kind, either. She finds his briskness funny, but he doesn't always answer. When she's tapped into her Highest Self, we always say something to her, because we want her to feel good. We want her to be lifted up and we want her to know that she is doing a fantastic job. At the same point Archangel Michael isn't worried about making her feel good and so he doesn't always respond.

One of the tasks the psychic gave to Kim in one of their sessions was to imagine a 12-member board of directors and imagine who would sit on that board. She said to imagine them all around a giant board table in the sky and to put herself at the head of the table. The psychic told Kim to pose them questions. Kim is still building who she wants at the table. She has met a couple of her guides. There's Larry the bus driver, who drives the bus of her life—though he has never shown Kim the map. There's a Sprite named Joy, who really resembles Joy from the movie *Inside Out* with blue hair and faint yellow body, only instead of being as tall as the other emotions like in the movie, Joy in Kim's head is very tiny, more like Tinkerbell, and Kim's Joy has wings and flies like Tinkerbell too. Kim knows Athena, the goddess of war, sits at the table, as does Diana, the goddess of the hunt and the moon. Joan of Arc is there, as well as Archangel Michael. She's pretty sure there's a Norse god that sits at the table too, but she knows that it's not Odin, and it's not Thor. She keeps thinking that she needs to read Norse mythology again, which she used to adore when she was in middle school.

Joan of Arc wants nothing to do with questions about boys, rolls her eyes, and says, "I don't know why we have to talk about this" in a French accent. Diana gets dreamy and gets it completely and Athena is mildly temperate around it because she has had her own trysts and understands.

Kim likes sitting at the head of the board and asking the board members questions because she knows that she's getting a balanced view, rather than just tapping into her Highest Self.

Can we give this challenge to you, dear reader? Who sits at your board? Do you tap into these board members when you Automatic Write? Do you make them a member of your team and reach out to them for guidance when you are uncertain, as Kim does?

So, how do you do this automatic writing thing?

You just sit down and start writing even if you don't know what to write. You put your pen to paper, or fingers to keyboard, and start with something like, "I don't know what to write. I don't know what I'm writing. My pen against the paper right now / My fingers on top of the keys. This is totally pointless and a waste of time."

Eventually if you go back and read, words will have come out too.

Words we want you to hear:

Do you know how loved you are? Do you know how fabulous you are? We wish you could see your value and your worth. We wish you could see how much you have to offer this world and how great you are. How much you have inside of you, that you are only waiting to tap open, and tap into. There is so much potential inside of you. Inside of you is the potential to open galaxies and to open the Universe and to give love unconditionally and without regard. There is flow and there is ease and there is this thing that

Kim struggles with called Release and Allow. There is Release and Allow inside of you, instead of resistance, and blockages, and hold ups, and weights, and what ifs. There are yes'es. There are amens. There are all the possibilities of everything wrapped up in there.

These are the words we want you to find in automatic writing. These are words that make you feel good, and alive, and whole, and blessed. Words that let you know that you are not alone and that you are seen. Words that make everything different.

Even if you just start with the line, "What do I need to know today?," we will tell you: You are lovely. You are wrapped up in potential. Your heart is beautiful and your love is true. There is happiness here for you in this lifetime and you don't have to wait. You just have to choose it. Your thoughts may be causing you problems and if you choose a thought that makes you feel better, you *will* feel better. Allow us to show you how you have abundance inside of your pinky; how you have abundance in your feet. You just don't know where to place your feet to make that happiness grow. You think your footsteps are no good, but inside of you, you hold potentials for drastic joy and overwhelming bliss.

These are the words we want to give you and this is what we hope you will find when you step into the practice of writing our words out to yourself. Kim has learned how good it feels.

So often this Earth-world is full of cutting down, being cruel, and being mean. That is no way to live. Yes! Amen! Huh-zah!! and Hope. These are words that inspire real living.

This is very important and we want you to hear this, dear reader. So, please, if you don't get anything out of all of these words we have shared, may these be the words that stick with you the most: If you, in any way, get words that make you feel small, belittled, insulted, yucky, pressured, put down—*these are not your intuition.* You may have tapped into your judgy ego or a low-level spirit. Stop immediately. Calibrate—in other words, recenter yourself. Ground. Meditate. Put on happy, uplifting, high-vibration music if grounding and meditating do not work. And then, when you are in a better mindset, start over.

If you feel encouraged, loved, supported, buoyed up, and seen—then, these are the words, ideas, insights to pay attention to.

Michael Sandler, in his book *AWE: The Automatic Writing Experience,* states that you should go back and reread the words you wrote in the morning back to yourself at night.

Lee Harris in his training on how to channel says that once you sit down and get words from your guides written down— words that uplift and encourage—to sit with them for a couple of days. To go back and read them, and re-read them. Let them simmer and stew inside your being, like one lets a crockpot linger. He says that the words are there, not for a quick fix, but for a lengthy pull, a long ponder, a deep insightful lingering.

Kim goes through fits of doing Automatic Writing every morning, like Morning Pages, the practice suggested in *The Vein of Gold* or *The Artist's Way* by Julia Cameron. Lee Harris suggests that, no, you only do it once a week and chew on the words like a cow chewing its cud—a long slow process. Michael Sandler says to do it every day—write in the morning and reread the words at night before going to sleep.

Really, it is on you to decide how this practice fits into your life. What the timeframes are: daily, weekly, bi-weekly, monthly. That is up to you and your practice. But it can be such a rich experience of inspiration and insight. A rich experience of being seen and feeling known. It might be challenging at first, with the fear of a blank page and what to fill it with? But once you ground down and tap into your Source, and do that hard practice of Release and Allow, the words will come. Even if it's slow at first, they will come.

We also want to talk to you, dear reader, *briefly*, about timing.

Timing is different in our time and your time. Earth time is linear. Our time is NOW. It's all happening NOW. Kim is married NOW. Kim is living on the coast NOW. Only, none of those things are true as she is typing this out in her linear timeline on Earth. She doesn't see it in her present, in her NOW and so she doubts the veracity of our words. Please believe us. Our words are truth—let them be hope. Let them ring true. Allow them a place in your heart to create the life of joy you want to see in this land.

As we close this chapter on automatic writing, it's important to remember that sometimes, the answers we receive may not align with what we expect to see in our physical reality. Like Kim, you may find yourself frustrated when what you're told doesn't materialize immediately, but trust that the Universe is working on a different timeline. The key is to remain open and to sit with the messages you receive.

Now that you've explored how to connect through writing, the next chapter will guide you through another critical skill: learning what to do when things go wrong. How do you recalibrate when you misinterpret the signs or feel disconnected from Source? We'll delve into techniques to ask for signs and refine your practice, ensuring that even in moments of doubt, you continue to move forward with trust and grace.

Exercise 5: Meditation for Preparing to Automatic Write

This meditation can be used anytime you need to focus, shift your mood, or bring yourself back to a grounded center. It's rooted in mindfulness-based stress reduction (MBSR) practices, making it ideal for use before automatic writing, as a foundation for your own meditation journey, or whenever you need a moment of calm.

Start by sitting in a comfortable position with your feet flat on the floor and your hands resting in your lap—either folded or relaxed, whichever feels right to you. Allow your shoulders to soften, letting your arms hang loosely like limp noodles. Begin by noticing where your breath is within your body, and gently encourage it to drop down into your lower belly.

Now, bring your attention to your headspace. You might try a technique suggested by Vishen Lakhiani from Mindvalley, where you imagine looking upward at a 45-degree angle as if there's a movie screen in front of you. But, for now, simply allow yourself to be present, letting your thoughts come and go without attachment.

If you're struggling to focus and find your thoughts overwhelming, imagine a river. Place each thought on a leaf and watch it float downstream. Some leaves might linger along the riverbank, especially if the thought is one you dwell on often. But as you continue watching, you'll notice that even these leaves eventually move along with the current.

Traditional MBSR asks you to focus solely on your breath, without any added imagery. But because our minds tend to get restless, it's okay to use these visualizations if it helps you stay engaged.

If you're feeling anxious or stressed, take a moment to notice where those emotions reside in your body. Is it in your throat?

Your chest? Behind your eyes? Are you furrowing your brow? Imagine those feelings gently shedding away, like a bird molting its feathers or an animal shedding its fur. You're not losing anything essential—just releasing the extra weight you don't need.

Once you've reached a calmer, more grounded space, you're ready to open your computer, take out your journal, and begin asking the questions that matter to you.

We're excited for you as you embark on this journey.

Chapter Six

What to Do When You Get It "Wrong"

We've all had those moments when we **know** something deep inside, only for the world to prove us wrong—or so it seems. In this chapter, we'll dive into what happens when intuition leads us to a dead end, or at least, that's how it feels. Using Kim's story as a guide, we'll explore the emotional and psychological effects of having your intuition seemingly fail you and how to navigate those moments with grace.

    The specific tool this chapter aims to teach is **navigating intuitive missteps with resilience.** Often, the ego gets involved, distorting the messages of intuition, leading to feelings of self-doubt and frustration. Through this chapter, you'll learn techniques to better process the times when your intuition doesn't align with reality and how to use those experiences as opportunities for growth, rather than proof that your inner knowing is faulty.

Kim was standing at her kitchen sink in August of 2023 doing the dishes, listening to Heather Alice Shea give an intuition training. As Kim was doing the dishes, she got a knowing, unlike any she had ever received, that came up from the ground, shot up her legs, moved up her entire body, and started to make her shake with the vibration of it. She received a knowing that was fact-checkable. She could look online and find out whether or not this thing was true or not. It was a thing of public record, and so she looked online and didn't see any record of it. She looked again a couple of days later, and still not present.

 Later while she was processing her experience of the moment where Source gave her an experience of one thing and the present reality of the moment where there was not any indication that it was true, she was in bed, half awake and half asleep. Her left brain and her right brain were arguing with each other. Her left brain, her ego, was telling her, "Your intuition is full of nonsense and why do we even listen to it? When are you going to learn it's full of lies? It says things that aren't true at all, and you believe it all the time and then you get hurt." It just continued giving her a hard time, "You are going to say whatever you need to say to yourself in order to justify listening to your intuition. You don't get it. It hurts us over and over and you just keep listening to it." Her ego was really mean to Kim, like really mean, and that might have made her cry more than having this overwhelming experience not be validated by public record.

 Kim had the opportunity to share this with Heather Alice Shea and Heather laughed so hard. She just sympathetically laughed and said, "Yes, this is what we do. We hear things. We try to check whether or not it's true. Then when it's not true or it's not true yet, we make up some story about it."

Chapter Six

There was a moment where Kim had a job interview that a friend helped her get. She was informed that she didn't get the position. She texted a different person and told him that she didn't get the job.

He texted back and said, "Are you upset?"

Her response was one word, "Yup."

A little later in the day, the friend showed up in her office with a cookie and Kim closed her office door.

They spoke for a couple of minutes.

One of the things Kim said to the friend was, "I'm hopeful for so many things. Yes, I was really, really hoping for this job and, because I didn't get it, it makes me wonder what are the other things that I'm really, really hopeful for that I'm not going to get? What are the other things that I'm standing in manifestation for that just aren't going to come together for me?"

We want to acknowledge how hard that can be, because we know the disappointment of hope deferred.

We understand the feelings of loss and upset and even possible betrayal when something doesn't come together the way that you think it's supposed to based on your intuition. Or the way you would hope it to. Sometimes it's just a "not yet," and sometimes it's a "no forever," and sometimes you might get the sense that you're really supposed to have this thing, like a job or a guy or a girl or a house or a car, and then it all falls apart like a sandcastle in a wave.

Kim was recently speaking to a friend who said that she was about to close on a 300-acre farm in Georgia that would have given her the fulfillment of her dream of creating a retreat center, and it fell apart. She really believed this is where she was supposed to be and domino after domino after domino fell over, and over, and over to prove that this wasn't the right property for her and her family. She said if it had happened a couple of years ago, she would have been a mess—not understanding and railing at the guides and railing at the Universe for not making it happen, for making her believe that she was supposed to have something she wasn't going to have. She said in this moment, in this version of now, she had peace and was able to let the property go.

Cristina Leeson says that there is free will and there is destiny. Some things are just meant to be, like they're fated. Then there are other things where free will comes in and mucks it all up. If it's destined, it will come back around again. Cristina said she had the opportunity to meet her husband five years before she did. She was taking a tour of a cosmetology school, and her husband was upstairs in classes while she was on that tour. She went to a different school to study. But if she had chosen the one she was on a tour of that day, she would have met the man she eventually married five years sooner.

Kim saw a man she would come to love passionately three years before she met him. They were both in the same coffee shop. She noticed him for sure. He was adorable and she was definitely attracted to him. But she decided to not talk to him for a number of different reasons. She let him leave without pulling his attention to her—she was in her masters for Social Work at that time, somewhere in the 2013/2014 school year. She graduated in spring of 2014, got a job, stayed there for two years, and fought her way into a hospital job part-time, and then took a full-time position in that same hospital in September of 2016. One day after being in the full-time role for a little while, walking down the hallway, the same man from the coffee shop was walking toward her and they met. It took her a long time to realize he was the man from the coffee shop—but they were fated to know each other.

Chapter Six

Remember the job Kim wanted—the private boarding school job that she used a snail and a caterpillar to try to see if she would get it? She saw a caterpillar and a snail in 24 hours as she requested. Then, all summer, there were snails under the garden hose. Kim took that to mean to continue to hope for that position. Cristina Leeson, at that time, told Kim, "You know, Kim, I've seen it where they were supposed to hire someone—in this instance, you—and they hire someone else because of free will. Then the person they hire doesn't work out, and then they might come back to you, if you are really the one who is supposed to have the job." In this instance, they didn't come back to me, and I already explained about my dad's health and why that was a good thing.

People have the right to choose. Free will takes over and people have the right to choose to go in the direction in which they're supposed to go or not.

We challenge you to think of a childhood dream. We challenge you to think of a desire you've had for a very long time that you squashed.

Now we want you to close your eyes, if you are in a space that is safe to do so, and we want you to imagine the kindest person in your family asking you to do the thing that you had a desire to do a long time ago. So, imagine the conversation. They ask you to go do the things that will create the dream in your life. And that person asks for a response from you—a yes you will, or a no you won't. Please feel that response, that yes or that no in your body. Does it feel good or does it feel bad? Where do those feelings sit in your body?

That decision, in this hypothetical, is free will. You get to decide your future and the direction you will take.

(But is this hypothetical? Did you just say yes or no to a childhood dream? Did you just make a major life decision and what does that mean for the next couple of days, weeks, months of your life? Or even more meaningful, what does that mean for the rest of your life?)

A Course in Miracles says that you can be the one who receives a miracle or you can be the one who creates miracles for other people. Both are possible at the same time, even. While you're waiting for your big YES, and your big breakthrough, and your big change, and your big hopes, and your big dreams to come into your current reality, remember there is other work to be done too. Just because what you're seeing in the natural may not be what you want for your future doesn't mean your future isn't possible. It certainly doesn't mean your intuition has steered you wrong.

Your intuition will help you grow that future and your intuition will help you create that future.

Let's talk about how.

The truth is, intuition isn't about always getting it "right" in the eyes of the external world. It's about learning, growing, and adjusting to the subtle energies and signals that guide you. It's about trusting the process, even when outcomes don't match expectations. As we move into the next chapter, we'll explore how to apply intuition effectively and why it's essential to understand its role in your decision-making process. Understanding when to listen and when to adjust helps us lean into our deeper knowing with greater wisdom. Ready to dive into how to make this a practical tool in your life? Next up: Application and Why There's a Need to Know Your Intuition.

Exercise 6: Meditation to Talk to a Guide/Spirit About Any Burning Life Question

Find a comfortable seated position with your feet flat on the floor, especially if you're seated in a chair. If you're lying down in bed, go ahead and allow yourself to sink into the surface, like a puddle.

For those seated, sit tall by stacking your vertebrae one by one, supporting yourself. Then let your shoulders drop, relax your hands in your lap, and settle into this space.

Begin by focusing on your breath. Notice it in your belly, along your nostrils, or wherever you feel it most. No need for expectations—just allow the day's tension to slip away as you settle into peaceful stillness.

Imagine yourself on a quiet beach with gentle waves rolling in. It might be nighttime, with a soft moonlit glow dancing on the water. Take in the simplicity of the scene: just the sound of the waves, the feel of the cool sand beneath your feet, and the dunes behind you. It's just you and this serene beach.

Now, notice an elevator to your right. It's one of those old-fashioned types. It wasn't there before, but it's here now. Walk over and press the button, stepping inside. Take a moment to notice the numbers on the panel. Which number do you feel drawn to press? Remember that number.

As you press the button, the elevator begins to descend. You drop down, deeper and deeper, until the doors open to reveal a clearing. In front of you is a bench by a pond. Sit down and look into the pond. Notice the color of the fish swimming below. When you can clearly see the color, you're ready to move on.

To your left, there's a gate. If you're not quite ready yet, that's okay—take your time. But when you are ready, stand up and begin walking toward the gate. Beyond it, go down the stairs. At the bottom of the stairs, follow the path of hard-packed earth that leads into a beautiful forest. The sun filters through the leaves, casting dappled light, and the sounds of birds and animals rustling fill the air. You feel completely safe here.

As you continue along the path, you notice an animal ahead. What kind of animal is it? It might be one that's expected in this kind of forest, or perhaps it's something more unusual. Just take note of it.

After you pass the animal, you arrive at a clearing where a cozy cabin stands. This place feels familiar, safe, and welcoming, like a personal retreat. Walk up the steps, open the door, and step inside. The space is neat, clean, and polished—everything is in its place, waiting for you.

Take in the details of the cabin. Is it large or small? Does it have stairs or perhaps a tiny-home feel? Notice any bookshelves, kitchens, or other rooms. There's a book on a shelf that catches your eye. Pull it off and examine the title and author. If it's unfamiliar, try to remember it for later.

As you explore the kitchen, you'll notice someone there. This might be a person, or maybe another being—you get to decide. If you don't recognize them, go ahead and ask, "Who are you?" Ask their name, and if you have a burning question, now is the time to ask. What answer do they give? Maybe they tell you that you already know the answer, or perhaps they offer exactly what you need to hear. If more questions come to mind, ask away. This is your safe space, and nothing is off-limits.

When you're ready, if it feels right, give them a hug, if that is comfortable for you. If you'd like to stay longer, feel free to pause here. When you're ready to move on, walk to the door, where you'll find a table. There's an item on it. Pick it up and place it in your left pocket. Then, reach into your right pocket and leave behind whatever you find there for later. Take note of the items you exchanged.

Step outside the cabin. The door closes and locks behind you effortlessly. No need to worry about it—it all happens smoothly. Walk back down the path, up the stairs, back past the bench with the fish, and step into the elevator. As the elevator rises, the doors open once more, and you find yourself back on the beach.

Now that the meditation is complete, you've gathered new insights. Take some time to note what you experienced. Record the number you pressed in the elevator, the color of the fish, the animal you encountered, the book you found, and your conversation in the kitchen. Also, write down the item you picked up and what you left behind.

Once you've reflected, you can explore the meanings behind these symbols. Consider looking up the spiritual significance of the number, animal, colors, and objects you encountered. You might even want to research the book or person you met if they're unfamiliar.

Thank you for sharing this practice with me.

Chapter Seven

Application and Why There's a Need to Know Your Intuition

Here in Chapter Seven, we take things even deeper. We've touched on the power of intuition in earlier chapters, but intuition isn't just a vague feeling or random hunch—it's your internal compass. Yet, so many of us walk through life on autopilot mode, letting subconscious habits and routines dictate our choices. Dr. Joe Dispenza describes this as "Subconscious Automatic Programming," where daily actions happen without much thought or conscious decision. In this chapter, we will uncover why it's so vital to break out of that automatic mode and intentionally connect with your intuition. By learning how to apply intuition in real-life decisions, you'll not only step into a more empowered life, but also one filled with clarity, purpose, and greater joy.

    The specific tool we'll focus on in this chapter is "how to actively engage your intuition in your daily decision-making process." You'll learn practical steps to move out of autopilot, recognize resistance, and trust the insights your intuition provides—even when those insights lead you into uncomfortable territory. It's time to go beyond simply hearing your inner voice and start taking action in alignment with it.

Dr. Joe Dispenza, in his book *Breaking the Habit of Being Ourselves,* says that most human action in any given day is because of Subconscious Automatic Programming. You see it from the moment you step out of bed and you walk to the bathroom. You follow your morning routine without thinking and sometimes you don't even fully wake up until you are somewhere down the highway in your car, driving down the road, and on your way to work. Sometimes you don't even wake up until you get to work. When Kim was teaching, there were days that she didn't even start talking until she got to work and the first person she spoke to were her colleagues. It was in these conversations when her brain started to engage. Some of her colleagues knew this about her and would actually like to pick on her and say things to her intentionally to get her to have to give intelligible morning thoughts.

If there's a detour on the way to work or there's a change in the pattern that is unexpected, the body has a reaction and that causes frustration and anger. When a head, or better stated, the ego, decides that it wants to go on a diet and the body is not in line, the head starts to get thoughts that are unusual: "You're starving us," "We're going to die!" "What will we eat when we go out to order?" "How will this work?" "You can't do this to us!" "It's all over now!" "You hate us!" "We know you hate us!"

In reality, yes, the ego makes some decisions (or it really likes to think it does), but most of the time it is the body that makes the normal everyday processes happen. This is how you wind up on the couch every night watching TV, rather than going out and doing something else. This is how you get stuck in ruts after three years and you look around and think, "How do I still work here?" and "How is this still my life?" Sometimes you allow those around you and their priorities to be more important than your priorities, as well.

Let us be honest with you, the job of your intuition is to wake you up and make you notice that there is more to this life than you are living. You have a purpose. You have drive. You have desire. So many of you have pressed down purpose, drive, and desire.

Melanie Warner says only 20% of the people on earth have found their purpose in life and feel like they're doing what they are meant to do. That is a lot of people who are sleepwalking through their lives—80% of Earth's population to be exact. That is a lot of people functioning solely on subconscious automatic programming.

This lifetime is so, so, so, short.

Kim had cancer. Did you, dear reader, know that? Kim had cancer and wrote a book about it: *What the Doctors Don't Tell You: One Woman's Journey Through Hodgkin's Lymphoma*. When Kim was done with treatment, she looked around at her life, the choices she had made, where she was. At that time, she was living in Newark, Delaware at her mentor and his wife's home, teaching in a little town called Northeast in Maryland in Cecil County. She was actively involved in a church and, to be honest, she was probably clinically depressed. She was definitely struggling with a panic disorder with the onset of PTS of a cancer diagnosis.

There were parts of her life that felt alive post cancer—she was speaking to one of the therapists shortly after cancer. (As a general note about therapists—think of first and second appointments with a therapist like you would a date. If you aren't comfortable with them, you owe them nothing. Feel free to move on and find a person you resonate and connect with. You won't grow and heal in a weird, awkward, or uncomfortable therapist situation.) She didn't stick with him, but she worked with him for a short while. She told him that she felt like she was supposed to have a bigger life. She always felt like she was supposed to be a speaker and that she was supposed to have these big life dreams fulfilled. This therapist said, "Not everybody feels that way." He said that lots of people don't want to be public speakers and don't want to be writers and don't want to be known. He said many people just want quiet lives filled with family and friends. It took her twelve years after this moment to finally be ready to open the doors to what *big* might mean in her life.

So, dear reader, please don't wait twelve years for a post-traumatic event like Kim did, not to mention, then 30-something years of life leading up to diagnosis.

We ask you what the poet Mary Oliver asks, "Tell me, what is it you plan to do with your one wild and precious life?"

Dear reader, what do you want in this life? What do you want to create? What do you want to see in this lifetime? What dreams have you put on the shelf and ignored? What dreams have you said "No" to?

Cristina Leeson said that you have to say "Yes" when opportunities come forward and you are asked to step into them. You are being asked to be bold.

If you say, "No," you stay stuck.

If you say, "Yes," you say yes to adventure, change, opportunity, and growth.

If you say, "No," you may get another chance to say "Yes" down the road of life, but then, you might not. You may only get that one opportunity to say "Yes."

Chapter Seven

Recently Kim has been given a couple of opportunities that have been very large and the timeline to decide was literally a night, or that moment. In one instance, there were only so many slots and when they were filled, they were filled. Other people could have gotten there first and taken the opportunity away from her. In another instance, the deadline was three days away and she was about to have major surgery to have her gallbladder removed and there was no time to decide. It was either, "Yes," or, "No," in that moment.

Kim has learned a couple of things in the past couple of weeks: If you want an opportunity to play in the "game," if you want an opportunity to be in a room, if you want an opportunity to be seen, you have to say, "Yes."

For a long time, Kim played small. For a long time, she didn't feel that she had what it took inside of her to be a player on a big stage. She always took support roles. As they say in the movie *The Holiday*, she played the role of the best friend in her own life.

There is a shift that has to happen inside of you in order to make you comfortable to be seen, especially if you've been in hiding, especially if you've been saying "No."

Resistance is feeling like an invisible wall separates you from the situations and circumstances you want to create in your life. Resistance feels like you are closed in. Resistance feels tight. Resistance feels uncomfortable. Resistance feels like there's a blockage between you and the thing you want.

Remember those Jericho Walls we talked about earlier? All of that could be applied here when talking about resistance.

Kim recently had to buy plane tickets to California. She had been putting it off. In fact, someone was even inquiring about her itinerary—people she was supposed to be working with when she was out there. So, because the deadline to buy them had come and gone, she sat down to purchase them. No more procrastination! Only when she stood up from the purchasing, she was slammed with a wall of resistance. She felt terrible. She felt like she had made a giant mistake. She felt overwhelmed and even a little nauseated. She did what she does to get rid of resistance. She breathed, looked at the feelings of it, and addressed them head on. There's a little more to it than that, but yes, she felt the walls of resistance come down. Then she wondered about all that she was doing: signing up to work with a new business coach, writing this book, agreeing to be on a PBS TV show, going on NBC in California, and agreeing to be a sponsor of the 2024 Emmy Suites. How was it that it was the plane tickets that took her out? But her ego saw that as the thing to keep her safe. If she didn't fly to California, she couldn't do all of the other things either.

One morning in April 2024, Kim got up in the morning and walked out of her house. She broke out of her subconscious automatic programming to realize that everything felt open. It felt like anything was possible. It felt spacious and exciting and joyous. It felt like possibility, a YES! and a thank goodness!

Kim knew in that moment she had leveled up. She didn't know what the exact future looked like, or what would manifest, or what would be brought in, or how this would change her circumstances, or how things would be different in the future. She just knew she felt different and was excited to be different.

This is available to you.

A wild adventurous life is open before you.

Something different, and bold, and big with a giant Yes! and Amen! attached to it.

Are you willing to step out and step forward and be brave to hear your intuition and to allow it to guide you to new lands and new open waters? To whatever it is that makes your heart sing with the possibility of joy and potential?

Are you willing to be brave?

Are you willing to learn how your intuition speaks to you?

What will it take to find, hear, see, and trust your intuition? Are you willing to do the work? Are you willing to pay the cost of not doing so? Not learning and growing in this area means more of the same.

Esther Hicks says that humans are always pressing into the next better thing, the next better feeling thought, the next better idea, the next better…. Always the next better.

That is Kim's dream for you too. What is next and better for you? What will you allow yourself to create in your life by allowing your intuition to take a more important role, a more center-stage position in your decision-making? What does possibility look like for you? And feel like? And sound like?

Now, allow your intuition to help you create that in your life.

Chapter Eight

Living Intuitively and Boldly— The Wrap-Up

Congratulations! You've come a long way. As we reach the end of this journey together, it's time to reflect on everything you've learned about intuition and how it can become the driving force in your life. Throughout this book, we've explored the nature of intuition, its truths, and the ways it can sometimes lead us down unexpected paths. We've also discussed how to recognize when you're on autopilot and how essential it is to apply intuition in real-time decisions. Now, it's time to embrace the ultimate challenge: living boldly with your intuition as your guide.

The key takeaway is this:

You have the power within you to create the life you want.

Your intuition is there to help you navigate, but only you can choose to listen and act. As we close, it's important to acknowledge that trusting your intuition won't always be easy. There will be moments of doubt, fear, and resistance. But it is in those very moments that your intuition is most valuable—it pulls you toward growth, transformation, and a life full of meaning.

Living intuitively means saying "**Yes**" to opportunities that light you up, while also being brave enough to let go of what no longer serves you. It means being present, awake, and intentional in your decisions. Most importantly, it means trusting yourself fully, even when the path ahead is unclear.

So, where do you go from here? You go wherever your intuition takes you. Whether it's pursuing a dream you've kept on the shelf for too long or simply making a small, brave step toward change, the adventure is yours to create.

This isn't the end—it's the beginning. The beginning of a new chapter in your life where you choose to live boldly, trust deeply, and act with intention. Remember, your intuition is always with you, guiding you toward the next best version of yourself. Now go out there and create the wild, precious life you've always wanted. You are ready.

The question is: Are you willing?

Exercise 7: Meditation for a Dream of an Ideal Future

Begin by finding your most comfortable seated position. You could be lying down, sitting on a cushion, or in a chair—whatever allows you to fully relax and focus. Settle in, pop your vertebrae one on top of the other, creating a nice alignment. Sit forward slightly if you're in a chair, with your feet flat on the floor, arms relaxed like limp noodles, and your hands floppy in your lap.

    Now, I want you to imagine yourself standing in front of your dream house. It doesn't matter where it is—that's entirely up to you. Maybe you're outside looking at it from the sidewalk, or perhaps you're inside, standing in the kitchen. Wherever you are, take in the view. This is your dream home, and you know every nook and cranny.

    Feel the gratitude rise up inside you for this space. Imagine your favorite rooms, the ones that bring you joy and comfort. My favorite room might be different from yours, so place yourself in your most cherished space. Notice the décor, the location, the energy that this house provides and supports in your life. Whether this house exists in reality or only in your imagination doesn't matter—what matters is how it feels to you.

    Now, move to the part of your dream home where you feel most comfortable, the place that's truly yours. Sink into it, whether it's a cozy chair, with a warm blanket, or perhaps there's a hot cup of tea, coffee, or cocoa waiting for you. Close your eyes in this space and let gratitude wash over you for the life you're living inside this dream home.

    Visualize your dream job. What does it look like? What kind of clothes do you wear? What does your workspace feel like? Who do you interact with? Are you the one calling the shots, or do you report to someone? Notice how your office or work environment feels. But more importantly, focus on how it feels to be you in this dream job. Swim in those feelings of accomplishment and fulfillment.

Now, let's talk about relationships. If you already have a partner, think about how you'd like that relationship to grow. What does the next level of connection look like for you both? If you're single, this part may feel a bit tricky, but go ahead and imagine growth with your ideal partner. You might not know exactly who they are, but visualize the kind of relationship you desire. It's okay to imagine a "stand-in" person. As many spiritual guides say, "This or something better," right? Whether you have someone in mind or not, know that the Universe is working in your favor.

Next, focus on your health. What does it feel like to be in peak health and vitality? Feel gratitude for your strong, healthy body, your vibrant energy, and your overall well-being.

If there's another area of your life that's calling for attention—be it spirituality, education, or anything else—bring that into focus now. What does growth in that area look like for you? Yes, feel the excitement of that vision coming to life.

And as you imagine all these elements—the home, the job, the relationships, the health—feel how good it is to be surrounded by these dreams. Swim in that feeling of possibility, like you're living in the future you've always desired.

Here's a secret: Your brain can't tell the difference between imagining your dream and remembering something that's already happened. Both live in the same place in your mind. So, by envisioning your future in this way, you're helping create it. You're stepping into that dream with ease, filling your aura with the energy of possibility and gratitude.

Chapter Eight

If you'd like to stay here a little longer, please do. You can keep building that bubble of joy and anticipation. Focus on your dreams, whether it's one or many. Let the feelings of having those dreams come true fill you up.

Thank you for trusting me to guide you through this powerful practice.

About the Author

Kim Beam is a transformative leader in the realm of intuition, guiding individuals to harness their innate insights to overcome obstacles. As a trailblazer for entrepreneurs and thought leaders, she facilitates growth and innovation within their respective fields.

With over 20 years of experience in developing her intuition and providing intuitive readings, Kim has transitioned from a passionate novice to a recognized expert. Her work has garnered acclaim, featured at the Emmy Gifting Suite 2024, in *Real Simple* (September 2024), *Success Savvy Magazine* (October 2024), *Medium* (November 2022, January 2023), *Canvas Rebel* (August 2023), *Vitality Digest* (October 2024), Insight Timer, and on NBC and WSFL.

Kim Beam holds Master's degrees in Social Work and Fine Arts, specializing in Creative Writing. With twelve years as a certified educator and over ten years as a social worker, she is passionate and empathetic. She sees what others overlook and shares insights that make people feel seen, heard, and supported on their journey. Her work is dedicated to helping others trust their inner guidance and live authentically.

Kim is also the author of *What the Doctors Don't Tell You: One Woman's Journey through Hodgkin's Lymphoma*.

Connect with Kim on social media at @IAmKimBeam on Facebook and @IamKimBeam Instagram, join her private Facebook group *Walk in Courage*, where she offers a different practice and teaching each week, listen to her podcast *Intuitive Insights with Kim Beam*, where she offers free intuitive readings, and join her weekly in her Zoom meetings where she gives free readings to some of the people present. To learn more, visit her at KimBeam.com or reach out at Info@KimBeam.com.

Share Your Thoughts: Leave a Review!

If this book has touched your heart or sparked a change in your life, I'd be deeply grateful if you could take a moment to share your experience.

Why Your Review Matters:
Your feedback helps others discover the insights and inspiration within these pages, and it supports me in continuing to share my journey and wisdom with the world.

How to Leave a Review:
Head over to Amazon or wherever you purchased this book, and leave an honest review. Your words truly make a difference and help others on their path to self-discovery and empowerment.

Thank you so much for your support and for being part of this journey. Your review means more than you know!

With heartfelt gratitude,

Kim

ABOUT DEFINING MOMENTS PRESS

Built for aspiring authors who are looking to share transformative ideas with others throughout the world, Defining Moments Press offers life coaches, healers, business professionals, and other non-fiction or self-help authors a comprehensive solution to getting their books published without breaking the bank or taking years. Defining Moments Press prides itself on bringing readers and authors together to find tools and solutions.

As an alternative to self-publishing or signing with a major publishing house, we offer full profits to our authors, low-priced author copies, and simple contract terms.

Most authors get stuck trying to navigate the technical end of publishing. The comprehensive publishing services offered by Defining Moments Press mean that your book will be designed by an experienced graphic artist, available in printed, hard copy format, and coded for all eBook readers, including the Kindle, iPad, Nook, and more.

We handle all the technical aspects of your book creation so you can spend more time focusing on your business that makes a difference for other people.

Defining Moments Press founder, publisher, and #1 bestselling author Melanie Warner has over 20 years of experience as a writer, publisher, master life coach, and accomplished entrepreneur.

You can learn more about Warner's innovative approach to self-publishing or take advantage of free training and education at: MyDefiningMoments.com.

DEFINING MOMENTS BOOK PUBLISHING

If you're like many authors, you have wanted to write a book for a long time, maybe you have even started a book ... but somehow, as hard as you have tried to make your book a priority, other things keep getting in the way.

Some authors have fears about their ability to write or whether anyone will value what they write or buy their book. For others, the challenge is making the time to write their book or having accountability to finish it.

It's not just finding the time and confidence to write that is an obstacle. Most authors get overwhelmed with the logistics of finding an editor, finding a support team, hiring an experienced designer, and figuring out all the technicalities of writing, publishing, marketing, and launching a book. Others have written a book and might have even published it but did not find a way to make it profitable.

For more information on how to participate in our next Defining Moments Author Training program, visit

www.MyDefiningMoments.com

Or email support@MyDefiningMoments.com

OTHER #1 BESTSELLING BOOKS BY DEFINING MOMENTS ™ PRESS

Defining Moments: Coping With the Loss of a Child—Melanie Warner

Defining Moments SOS: Stories of Survival—Melanie Warner and Amber Torres

Write your Bestselling Book in 8 Weeks or Less and Make a Profit—Even if No One Has Ever Heard of You—Melanie Warner

Become Brilliant: Roadmap From Fear to Courage—Shiran Cohen

Unspoken: Body Language and Human Behavior For Business—Shiran Cohen

Rise, Fight, Love, Repeat: Ignite Your Morning Fire—Jeff Wickersham

Life Mapping: Decoding the Blueprint of Your Soul—Karen Loenser

Ravens and Rainbows: A Mother-Daughter Story of Grit, Courage and Love After Death—L. Grey and Vanessa Lynn

Pivot You! 6 Powerful Steps to Thriving During Uncertain Times—Suzanne R. Sibilla

A Workforce Inspired: Tools to Manage Negativity and Support a Toxic-Free Workplace—Dolores Neira

Journey of 1000 Miles: A Musher and His Huskies' Journey on the Century-Old Klondike Trails—Hank DeBruin and Tanya McCready

7 Unstoppable Starting Powers: Powerful Strategies for Unparalleled Results From Your First Year as a New Leader—Olusegun Eleboda

Bouncing Back From Divorce With Vitality & Purpose: A Strategy For Dads—Nigel J. Smart, PhD

Focus on Jesus and Not the Storm: God's Non-negotiables to Christians in America—Keith Kelley

Stepping Out, Moving Forward: Songs and Devotions—Jacqueline O'Neil Kelley

Time Out for Time In: How Reconnecting With Yourself Can Help You Bond With Your Child in a Busy Word—Jerry Le

The Sacred Art of Off Mat Yoga: Whisper of Wisdom Forever—Shakti Barnhill

The Beauty of Change: The Fun Way for Women to Turn Pain Into Power & Purpose—Jean Amor Ramoran

From No Time to Free Time: 6 Steps to Work/Life Balance for Business Owners—Christoph Nauer

Self-Healing for Sexual Abuse Survivors: Tired of Just Surviving, Time to Thrive—Nickie V. Smith

Prepared Bible Study Lessons: Weekly Plans for Church Leaders—John W. Warner

Frog on a Lily Pad—Michael Lehre

How to Effectively Supercharge Your Career as a CEO—Giorgio Pasqualin

Rising From Unsustainable: Replacing Automobiles and Rockets—J.P. Sweeney

Food—Life's Gift for Healing: Simple, Delicious & Life-Saving Whole Food Plant-Based Solutions—Angel and Terry Grier

Harmonize All of You With All: The Leap Ahead in Self-Development—Artie Vipperla

Powerless to Powerful: How to Stop Living in Fear and Start Living Your Life—Kat Spencer

Living with Dirty Glasses: How to Clean those Dirty Glasses and Gain a Clearer Perspective Of Your Life—Leah Montani

The Road Back to You: Finding Your Way After Losing a Child to Suicide—Trish Simonson

Gavin Gone: Turning Pain into Purpose to Create a Legacy—Rita Gladding

The Health Nexus: TMJ, Sleep Apnea, and Facial Development, Causations and Treatment—Robert Perkins, DDS

Samantha Jean's Rainbow Dream: A Young Foster Girl's Adventure into the Colorful World of Fruits & Vegetables—AJ Autieri-Luciano

Live Your Truth: An Arab Man's Journey In Finding the Courage to Live His Truth As He Identifies as Gay and Coping with Mental Illness—David Rabadi

Unstoppable: A Parent's Survival Guide for Special Education Services with an IEP or 504 Plan—Raja B. Marhaba

Please, Excuse My Brave: Overcoming Fear and Living Out Your Purpose—Anisa Wesley

Drawing with Purpose: A Sketch Journal—Rick Alonzo

NY Coffee: Love Fulfilled in the Little Things—Craig Lieckfelt

Good Work: How Gen X and Millennials are the Dream Team for Doing Good When Collaborating—Erin Kate Whitcomb

Rescue Me: Guided Self-Healing for First Responders: Conquering Depression, Anxiety, PTSD & Moral Injury—David Hogan

Treasures In Grief: Discover 7 Spiritual Gifts Hidden in Your Pain—Lo Anne Mayer

We Three: Their Beginnings—Derek Drummond

Culture Spin—Kristy Wachter

Discover Your Inner Leader—Mamta Goyal

Grit, Growth and Gumption for Women: Three Keys To Lead Yourself and Others With Confidence—Tinsley English

Low Back Pain 3 Steps to Relief in 2 Minutes—Helene Bertrand

The Unified Way: Balancing Masculine & Feminine Powers as an Entrepreneur Utilizing HumanDesign.ai —Princella Stringer

EVERYTHING IS PERSONAL: Embracing Stewardship in the Workplace and Everyplace—Louis Roden

Choosing Your Perfect Tree: Tips from a Landscape Designer—Laural Roaldson

Transformative Path: 7 Steps To Personal Growth And Empowerment—Parveen Smith

THE CROOKED PATH IS PERFECT: FINDING YOUR POWER WITHIN—Satie Simon

The Classroom Formula: Mastering Classroom Management and Empowering Teachers for Success—Ramez Takawy

Presence: Self-Coaching Strategies to Ignite Your Authentic Leadership—Sheila R. Carmichael, MCC, MEd

Made in the USA
Middletown, DE
13 April 2025